South Head Sydney

and

The Origins of Watsons Bay

Robin Derricourt

South Head Sydney and The Origins of Watsons Bay

Copyright Robin Derricourt 2011

robin@derricourt.com

Published 2011 by Watsons Bay Association
Sydney, Australia

ISBN 978-0-646-56781-5

Design by Josephine Pajor-Markus, josie_sara@hotmail.com

COVER IMAGE Joseph Lycett 'View of the Heads at the entrance to Port Jackson', from *Views of Australia*, London, 1824.

Contents

Preface

This study of the early history of the South Head peninsula and Watsons Bay was undertaken between 2005 and 2011.

Among those to whom thanks are due for assistance in the preparation on this study are Val Attenbrow, Bruce Crosson, and the staff of the National Parks and Wildlife Service Hurstville. I acknowledge the assistance of staff at the Mitchell Library, the Local History Centre of Woollahra Library, and the Library of the University of New South Wales, where I have held honorary appointments in the School of History and Philosophy. All errors and omissions are the responsibility of the author.

Versions of some material included in this text have appeared elsewhere. I contributed to the online *Dictionary of Sydney* articles on Watsons Bay, Camp Cove, South Head, The Gap, Macquarie Lighthouse, the South Head Signal Station and HMAS Watson. That on Watsons Bay also appeared in *Sydney Journal* 1 (2) (2008), 117-125. An article 'Sydney's lookout and signal station' appeared in *Australian Heritage* 13 (2008), 12-15. A detailed discussion of some aspects of the area's history appeared as 'The South Head peninsula of Sydney Harbour: boundaries in space and time' in the *Journal of the Royal Australian Historical Society* 96 (1), (2010), 27-49. Illustrations prepared for that article by Negin Miri have been included in the present text. Grateful thanks are given to the State Library of New South Wales, the National Library of Australia and other organisations who have granted permission to include illustrations in this work.

Robin Derricourt

Watsons Bay
September 2011

1

Aboriginal South Head

The settlement of Watsons Bay represents the earliest European occupation on the peninsula that extends to South Head, marking the entrance of Port Jackson (Sydney Harbour) from the Tasman Sea. The area's importance and interest in the colonial history of Sydney is matched by its importance to preceding indigenous communities, using the economic resources provided by the landform and position of the South Head peninsula.

The South Head peninsula

The peninsula rises north from the beach at Bondi, and from the sand dunes behind it. The sandstone cliffs[1] facing the ocean ascend to a height of 90 metres above sea level and stretch for some 7 kilometres to the mouth of the natural harbour at Inner South Head. At its widest, the land descends just over 2 km west from the cliffs to meet the waters of Port Jackson (Sydney Harbour), so that the total area is no more than 5.9 square kilometres. A few small streams drain the peninsula into the harbour, emerging at sandy and mostly protected bays. Above the bays the natural vegetation of woodland extended back to the cliff top, until the impact of modern suburban settlement.

The land is separated from the rest of the Australian landmass by a low lying sandy area no higher than 20 metres above sea level, where the sand has blown inland from the beach at Bondi, linking to the sands of the harbour some 2.5 km away. This sandy patch has a similar width, narrowing to 1 km. Before European settlement it carried a sparse natural heathland vegetation of Banksia scrub, and could at times contain a flooded lagoon.[2] Lieutenant William Bradley, describing the first arrival of Europeans to settle in Sydney Cove noted how the entrance to Port Jackson was hidden:

> the best mark to know when you draw near it coming from the southward, is, some remarkable sandhills over a sandy bay 2 or 3 miles to the southward of the South Head, the shore from this bay to the South Head is high rocky cliffs.[3]

The sandstone – of quartz origin with shale inclusions – is one of the youngest of the sandstone deposits that have created the continent of Australia. It was laid down by ancient river systems when Australia was part of the great southern continent Gondwana, some time in excess of 200 million years ago.

The movements of the earth's plates bent and folded the sandstone levels and gave the region its warped form which was further weathered by wind and rain.

But just as water had laid down the rock, it was water which gave the landscape the appearance we recognise today. The ocean tides eroded the eastern side of the peninsula creating the towering cliffs. And on the west the Parramatta River slowly cut its river valley into the rock as it flowed into the sea. Just north of the peninsula it met with the flow of another river (today's Middle Harbour) flowing from the north.

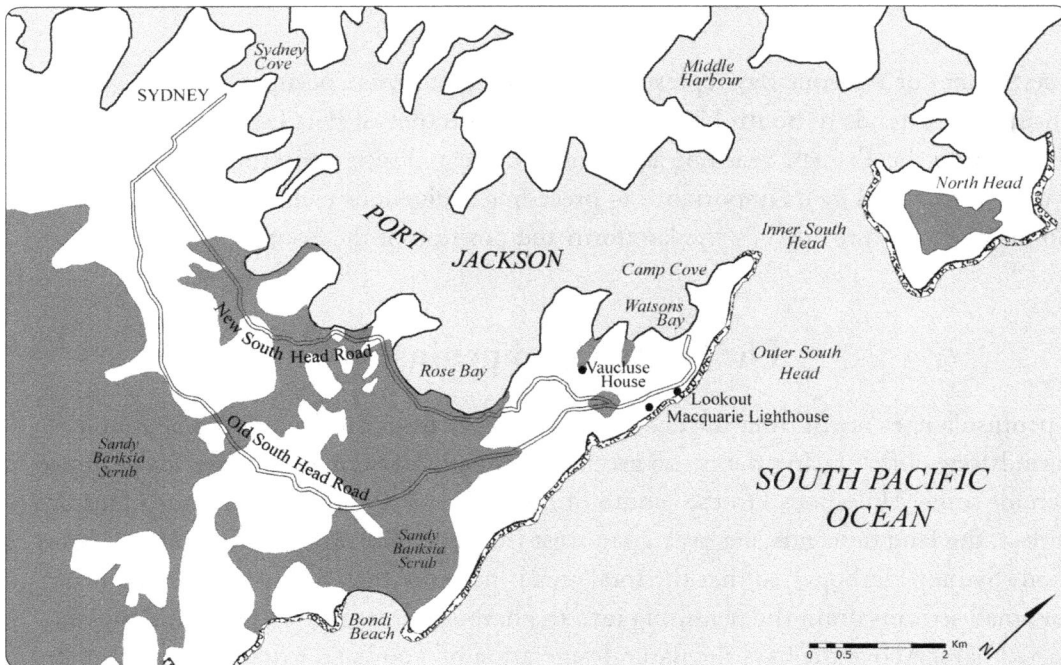

The South Head peninsula. The shaded area marks areas of sandy deposits.
SOURCE Derricourt, 'The South Head peninsula'.

The water of the combined rivers continued to cut more deeply into the sandstone bedrock until the tides of the sea could, in turn, add to the wave pressure on the area of the river mouth. And slowly the sea began to encroach on the river valley. Flooding it with sea water, eroding it with the daily pressure of tides, until the saline water of the ocean and the movements of the tides extended far inland, and the waters of the river became no longer drinkable by the land creatures. The peninsula became, as today, surrounded entirely by saltwater or by sand.

Major change came with the ice ages that affected the world for much of the last two million years. As the earth experienced colder periods the ice sheets at the poles grew and sea levels correspondingly fell. In warmer intervals the ice sheets melted and sea levels rose, at times above that of the present day. Within the last 130,000 years the sea levels may have risen up to 5 metres higher than today, which would have had only a minor effect on the peninsula, making it slightly smaller, covering today's beaches and reducing the width of the sandy area that separates the peninsula.

However at the heights of the glaciations, sea levels had fallen very significantly, creating a quite different landscape experienced by the first humans to reach the area.

By a little over 40,000 years ago[4] the first humans had reached Australia from the north. They spread relatively quickly but in small numbers around the Australian coast, exploiting the very diverse range of plant and animal foods. When they reached the Sydney area, the sea level was already some 50 metres or more below that of the present day. Today's cliffs from Bondi north were an escarpment looking out over a flat plain of sandy scrub, while the lower sea level meant that the Parramatta River had again reclaimed its valley and provided fresh water, flowing out into the sea across the sandy plain.

At the height of the recent ice age – some 18,000 years ago – sea level was as much as 130 metres below that of today, and the sea edge lay up to 15 km to the east of today's cliffs.[5] Below today's cliffs, in a climate cooler and drier than today's, extended a sandy plain which provided access to marine resources. However, for shelter in the harsher climate it was necessary to seek rock shelters around the coastal cliffs, locations which are now eroded by ocean waves.

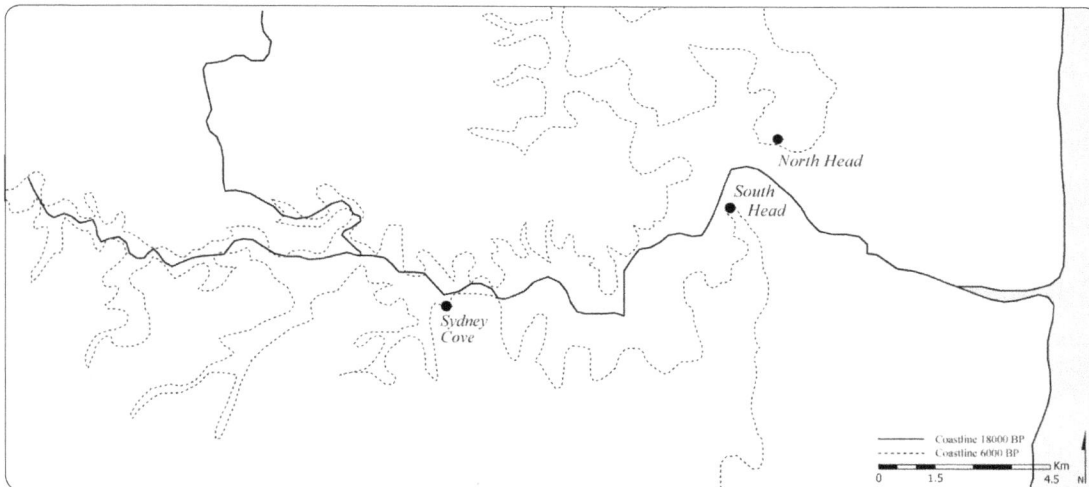

Coastline at 18,000 years ago.
SOURCE Derricourt, 'South Head Peninsula'

The bushland of today's peninsula provided hunting and food gathering opportunities for indigenous Australians settled on the freshwater river or using marine resources.

Between 10000 and 6500 years ago the sea levels rose and the river valley was again flooded. For the last 6500 years the topography was much as we see it today, with water levels at times 1-2 m higher, and small streams the only source of fresh water. At the harbour edge of the sandstone were water laid sandy beach deposits and at the height of the peninsula in Vaucluse lay a small area of wind blown marine sand.[6]

The overlying soils correspond broadly to the geology. On the peninsula all the soils are shallow but there is some contrast between the erosional soils of the upper more exposed areas and the colluvial soils of the west of the peninsula, echoed at South Head itself towards the harbour mouth.[7]

The appearance of the South Head peninsula in 1788.
SOURCE 'Entrance of Port Jackson 27 January 1788' William Bradley - Drawings from his journal 'A Voyage to New South Wales', Mitchell Library, State Library of NSW, Call number: Safe 1 / 14, Folio 10.

The natural vegetation of this area before European settlement followed the variation of geology and soils. The sandy area that linked the ocean at Bondi to the harbour at Rose Bay was covered by low heathland and Banksia Scrub,[8] today an endangered ecological community, best seen on North Head. This provided a relatively open landscape with sclerophyllous heath, scrub and low forest.[9] The area exposed by low sea level may have extended this vegetation, or may have supported a lower coastal heath vegetation. The isolated high patch of marine sands in Vaucluse probably carried a patch of coastal dune heath.[10]

The rest of the peninsula had a natural vegetation of mixed Eucalypt forest of the Sydney Sandstone Complex[11] – ranging from tall forest with denser undergrowth on the slopes and gullies leading into the harbour, and more open, lower, sparse woodland on the exposed cliff and ridge tops.[12] The most exposed cliff tops carried only a heath flora.[13] This varied range of flora did of course provide for human settlement a varied range of edible plant foods and fauna.[14]

Indigenous human settlement

The first Aboriginal settlement of the area had access to the plain that extended below the cliffs and bordered the river flowing eastward of today's South Head. There they could exploit freshwater, estuarine and marine resources.[15]

After the modern landscape was established, the peninsula provided a base for exploiting the fish and shellfish of Port Jackson (Sydney Harbour), supplemented by plant foods and meat from land fauna.

Bondi Beach gives the best access to marine resources and in the period of lower sea levels would have provided a convenient route to the coastal plains. This importance is reflected in archaeological finds from the area. To the south of the beach is a rock shelter with shell midden deposits.[16] Stone axes and a skull had been found exposed by the sand behind the beach.[17] The major site was an open area of scattered stone artefacts in the sandhills of North Bondi, reflecting a camp site with industrial activity, exposed by erosion in 1900.[18] The location is close to a diatreme – a volcanic pipe composed of brecchia and basalt. More significantly it is at an ecological boundary – an ecotone – where the sandy stretch behind Bondi meets the rocky peninsular and is close to the ocean.

The report of these finds noted artefacts of quartz, chert, quartzite and metamorphic rocks, suggesting raw materials from a wide area. Styles included the backed blade called a Bondi point,[19] and the pioneer archaeologist Fred McCarthy[20] considered this the type site of a *Bondaian* industrial tradition that predated the immediately pre-European stage; the Bondi point being not in use in this area at the time of European contact. The Bondi point seems common after around 3000 years ago but faded out of use in the region by about 650 years ago.[21]

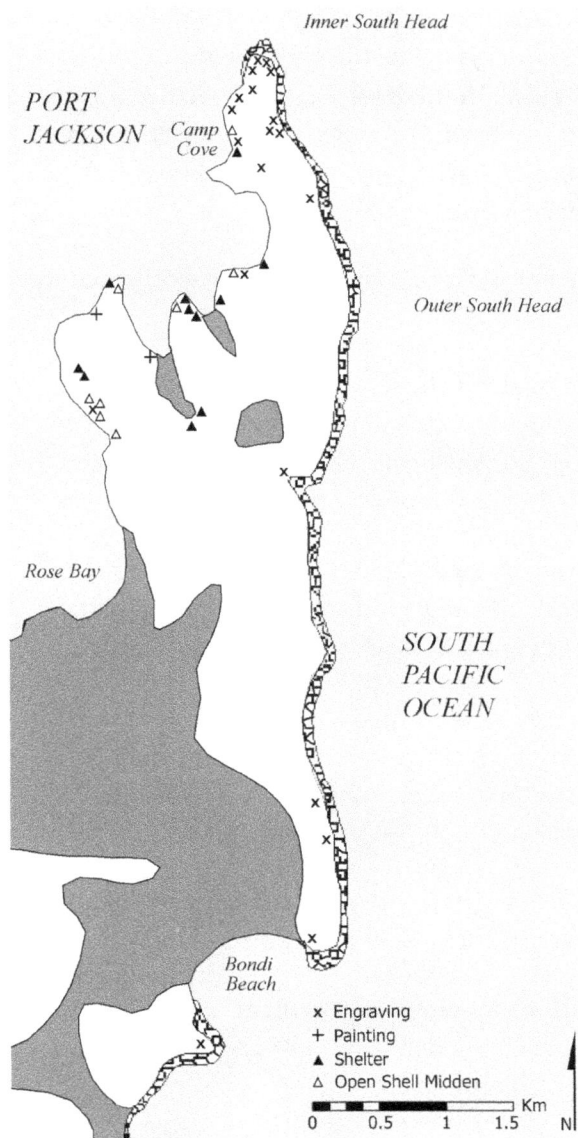

x Engraving
+ Painting
▲ Shelter
△ Open Shell Midden

0   0.5   1   1.5   Km   N

The archaeological evidence is good for the period before European settlement. There are a number of low rock shelters in the South Head peninsula, close enough to the waters of Port Jackson to be a base from which fish and shellfish could be acquired. None of these were large enough to be a long-term home base for a family or clan, but they would provide a base for a day and some for an overnight stay for a fishing or shell-collecting expedition. Some have paintings within them.

The best example is the shelter at Mount Trefle[22] near Nielsen Park Vaucluse. Excavated in the early 1990s by archaeologist Val Attenbrow, the site was a shelter less than 2 metres high with a shallow occupation deposition and eroded scatters below, carrying a dense deposit of stone artefacts, shellfish remains, fish

Archaeological sites of settlement for the period before 1788. The shaded areas mark sandy soils.
SOURCE Derricourt, 'South Head Peninsula'

bones and other fauna. Radiocarbon dating showed the site was in use from around 1300 years ago (the 8th century AD) as a base for food collecting. Two hand stencils in white within the shelter are of unknown age. The main fish remains were snapper, bream and wrasse with rare other species; and the emphasis seems to have been in catching immature snapper and bream in shallow waters. However a diverse range of fishing methods and strategies was employed.[23] The main shellfish were hairy mussel, rock oyster and black nerita. There was very little animal bone – in such a small isolated area it may have been virtually hunted out – with presence of kangaroo or wallaby, a mouse and some bird bones. The presence of rabbit, sheep and dog in the upper layers showed the cave was still used in European times. The paucity of terrestrial fauna emphasises the primary role of the site as a fishing camp. The stone artefacts were mainly of quartz.

Other deposits of shellfish, many associated with low shelters, have been identified in the coastal stretch between Rose Bay and Watsons Bay and we can assume many others have been destroyed by modern construction.

Close to the Mt Trefle site is another small shelter with shell deposit[24] while at nearby Milk Beach are several midden deposits – one is an open site, the others within and in front of small low shelters.[25] The dominant shellfish in these are hairy mussel, Sydney cockle, heavy turban as well as rock oyster, mud oyster, and a range of other occurrences. There was also said to be a site here with pecked engravings and grinding grooves.[26] A possible eroded midden lies a little further south in Hermit Bay.[27]

The area of Nielsen Park was formerly bisected by a stream called Shark Creek that led to a lagoon behind the beach.[28]

Not far from Mt Trefle and radiocarbon dated to about the same date, Hydrofoil Cave,[29] one of several overhangs at Bottle and Glass Point,[30] was also investigated by Attenbrow in 1990. This small rock shelter showed human use for shell collecting, with a wide range of species, especially turban, hairy mussel, black nerita and limpet shells.

In the same area, but now destroyed, was a group of three shelters with painted art.[31] This was recorded as white hand stencils, red ochre shields and a red ochre boomerang, with superimpositions of three painting stages. Another painted cave is near Vaucluse House on Olola Avenue[32] with two faint hand stencils.

Further east at Vaucluse Beach[33] is a shelter with both stone artefacts and European objects, and shells including periwinkle, limpet, turban, rock oyster, hairy mussel, Spengler's triton and black nerita.

There are a number of low shelters bordering Parsley Bay, with a shell deposit of unknown age.[34] In one of these were formerly visible two hand stencils.[35]

Other sites include a possible small shelter with rock oyster and cartrut at Gibsons Beach,[36] of uncertain date; a shelter with some shell midden deposit at Camp Cove[37] and an open site nearby.[38]

Just behind Camp Cove, in today's Victoria Street, two skeletons were discovered in 1963.[39] A police doctor identified these as 'aboriginal and several hundred years old' but no archaeological investigation seems to have taken place. The skeletons are described as perfectly preserved, and each skeleton had been laid on its back.

A local resident, William Francis Brown, who died in 1948, referred to an Aboriginal burial place in a sandy area a little to the south of the steps down to Camp Cove at the end of Cliff Street, and mentioned one body being seven feet long.[40]

The Australian Museum holds finds from the area. A ground basalt axe was located around 1885 in a midden of food refuse (presumably shellfish and fish bones) between the north end of Camp Cove and the freshwater lagoon.[41]

Another ground stone axe was dug up close to Diamond Bay between the South Head Cemetery and the cliffs,[42] and a basalt ground stone implement was reported from Rose Bay.[43] Three sandstone discs were found in a midden at an unknown location reported as Watsons Bay.[44]

Engravings

Rock engravings are found at a wider distribution of sites, not all linked directly to coastal resources. Most of these recorded in the classic work of W.D. Campbell in 1899[45] have been destroyed or eroded to minimal visibility.

On the Port Jackson side there were rock engravings in Bellevue Hill[46] and Point Piper,[47] near a shelter with shell midden deposit.

Waterside engravings of fish and shields have been reported near Milk Beach.[48] In Wentworth Street Vaucluse is an engraved site with a large fish and a boomerang.[49] Just west of Vaucluse House is an open surface with still visible pecked outlines of a man with headdress, a kangaroo (or wallaby) and what may be a fish, shark or whale.[50] There is a kangaroo on an open surface south of Vaucluse Bay.[51]

Rock engravings in the grounds of Vaucluse House
SOURCE Insites (Sydney, Historic Houses Trust) Autumn 2006

There are three separate sites between Gibsons Beach and Kutti Beach at Watsons Bay: one with a fish, one a man, and one with a turtle and man (or two humans), the latter in a rockshelter which may be that in Kutti Beach.[52]

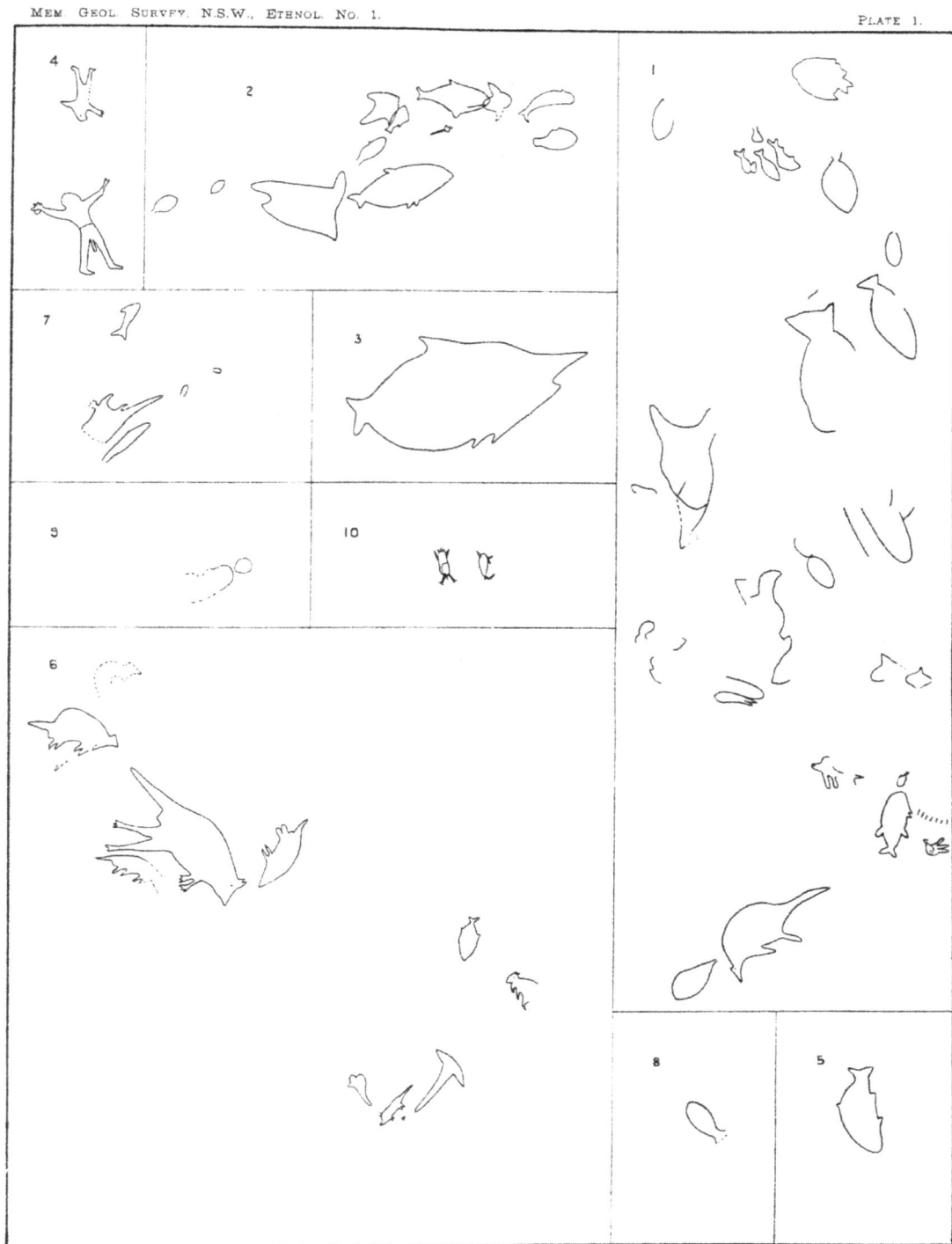

MEM. GEOL. SURVEY. N.S.W., ETHNOL. NO. 1.   PLATE 1.

Rock engravings at South Head and area
SOURCE Campbell, Aboriginal Carvings

There are comparable sites of rock engravings between Botany Bay and Bondi Beach and at the south of Bondi Beach is a whale (or shark) and a fish.[53]

North of Bondi Beach at Ben Buckler were a whale, turtle and eels.[54]

On the golf links here are the well known engravings[55] (recarved in modern times) of human figures, boomerangs, and numerous maritime fauna. These include whale, porpoise, fish, shark and octopus, with over 80 separate figures. Thus the greatest density of engravings is only a few hundred metres from the greatest density of earlier stone artefacts at the North Bondi settlement site.

Further north in Hugh Bamford Park was a warlike figure of a man.[56] At Diamond Bay are peck marked images and circular forms.[57]

Well studied though mostly now invisible are the rock engravings at South Head in Watsons Bay, the site of the earliest reports by Europeans of Aboriginal art in Australia.[58] They stretch along the cliff top, and along the areas accessible to Sydney Harbour, with a significant number at Inner South Head itself, which was a major Aboriginal fishing site. Subjects include humans, bandicoot, kangaroos and wallabies, and marine fauna – fish, whales, sharks – as well as geometric shapes.

Governor Phillip was moved to comment on the rock engravings in the very first year of European settlement in Sydney, 1788, when he reported:

> in the neighbourhood of Botany Bay and Port Jackson, the figures of animals, of shields, and weapons, and even of men, have been seen carved upon the rocks… Fish were often represented, and in one place the form of a large lizard… On the top of one of the hills, the figure of a man in the attitude usually assumed by them when they begin to dance…[59]

His companion Watkin Tench was less impressed, noting 'rock engravings of men and birds, very poorly cut'.[60] Copies were made in 1802 during Baudin's expedition to New South Wales.[61]

Sites visible a century ago have been eroded by weather; only those recarved in the period (as at Bondi) are now clearly visible. Recarving of sites may have been a long standing tradition. But the disappearance of engravings over a century does suggest those recorded by Campbell and others were of relatively recent origins. The engraving tradition in Sydney may extend far back, but sites older than a few hundred years are unlikely to be found in open locations.

The settlement sequence

The best interpretation of the human use of the South Head peninsula before European settlement would see it in three stages.

Firstly, before 6500 years ago, when sea levels were lower, it was a ridge open to occasional use by hunters and food gatherers from settlement sites now flooded by the ocean.

Some time within the period from about 5000 BP[62] onwards, during what archaeologists call the Australian Small Tool Tradition,[63] there was settlement at north Bondi Beach within reach of the diverse resources of the ocean, the harbour, the sandy heathland and the woodland of the South Head peninsula, whose animal and plant resources could be exploited for food. In particular this may reflect the greater exploitation of the coastal fringe that occurred from 3000-2000 years ago.[64] The disappearance of the Bondi point may mark an end to this phase.

From about 1600 years ago the Sydney region saw changes which may mark greater population density,[65] less long distance mobility, greater specialisation in land and resource use and the emergence of social and tribal groupings.[66] It is from this period that the other surviving sites in the peninsula belong: both shelter use and rock engravings. These changes are reflected in tool technology, including a greater development of fishing technology with a shift in coastal areas to more bone and shell implements and less focus on high quality stone tool production. Notable was the use of fish hooks made from shell in the last 700 years before European settlement.

There was clearly intensive use of the resources of Sydney Harbour and this concentrated occupation of the peninsula may in turn have reduced the survival of other land fauna, further strengthening the shift to fish and shellfish. Kohen[67] discusses density for Aboriginal populations and suggests an occupation pattern averaging around 1.2 persons per square kilometres, more than double that of the inland Cumberland Plain. But the much greater occupation of the South Head peninsula reflects the intensive use of coastal resources.

Aboriginal society and European contact

In many parts of the world, the first impact of Europeans was unrecorded: hunters, adventurers, traders, settlers, with literary records following on and recording a world already impacted by the changes these gradual contacts had already created. The Sydney region and Port Jackson region are unusual in that first contact between Europeans and indigenous people was the planned, mass arrival in 1788 of a large party of 1500 which included many who recorded their encounters and experiences in writing (and indeed in print) alongside the impacts which changed the indigenous societies for ever.

The very initial observations were therefore of the Aboriginal world of Port Jackson as it operated in the late 18th century. Thereafter observations have to be filtered and reinterpreted in the light of the impacts of European settlement, of which the smallpox outbreak of 1789 was the most immediate and dramatic.

The visibility and density of settlement in 1788 is striking. Lieutenant Ralph Clark noted, on entering Port Jackson on 26 January 1788 that he 'saw a great number of fires and a few Natives'.[68]

Daniel Southwell observed:

> They seldom appear in number exceeding 20 or 30, but once or twice 50 at least were in a company.... The shores everywhere by the seaside are plentifully covered with the shells of [great] variety, particularly oyster and many of them large. Most of them had evidently been cleared of their contents by the natives...[69]

Governor Phillip had a clear priority to open dialogue with the natives of Australia and avoid conflict as far as possible. The numbers seem to have surprised him. He observed their economy in which 'women fish from canoes, men strike [shell]fish from the rocks, and hunt'.[70] He reported:

> The natives are far more numerous than they were supposed to be. I think they cannot be less than fifteen hundred in Botany Bay, Port Jackson, and Broken Bay, including the intermediate coast.[71]

Further information on population density came from a journey Phillip took to Botany Bay then back up the coast. At a site on the coast somewhere south of Bondi he found a group of 212 people at a cove with 'the finest stream of fresh water'.[72] There was a further group of about 40 in a bay to the north. Such a large concentration must indicate some special occasion – perhaps even inspired by the arrival of the European settlers who clearly marked a threat to the indigenous economy.

> Governor Phillip had now determined to return to Port Jackson; but as he went, keeping for some time near the sea coast, he discovered a great number of the natives, apparently more than could belong to that district, assembled at the mouth of a cave. .... In less than three minutes the English party found itself surrounded by two hundred and twelve men ... Here was seen the finest stream of water that had hitherto been discovered in the country, but the cove into which it runs lies very open to the sea. When the natives saw that the English were going forward towards the next cove, one of them, an old man, made signs that he might be allowed to go first. He did so, and as soon as he had ascended the hill, called out, holding up both his hands... to signify to the natives in the next cove that they who were advancing were friends. The Governor's party did not, however, descend to that cove, but saw about forty men, so that, unless they had assembled themselves on some particular occasion, they must be more numerous in that part than had been before imagined.[73]

The harbour mouth itself was a major economic zone for Aboriginal fishing communities, approached from both South Head and the north of the harbour. Phillip noted women fishing in canoes and men in manufacturing:

> the men being chiefly occupied in making canoes, spears, fish-gigs, and the other articles that constitute their small stock of necessary implements[74]

with a count of some 67 in the canoes and 133 on the land, though these may have been on either side of the harbour mouth.[75]

South Head was a site of return visits by the officers of the First Fleet, as it marked not only the entrance to the Harbour but the most accessible site from which they could observe the ocean and coast down to Botany Bay. These visits encountered Aboriginal fishing parties. Hunter visited Camp Cove, site of first European landfall in Sydney Harbour just within the entrance, only two days after the settlement at Sydney Cove, and there he found three men, women and canoes.[76] Bradley's journal recorded:

> In course of the forenoon we went to a Cove within the Inner South Head (Camp Cove) where we were cordially received by 3 Men, who left their women sitting in a Canoe at the other end of the beach, we made a fire on shore and dined in the Boats, while our people were cooking the dinner, the natives were amongst them playing, looking at the Boat, manner of Cooking etc. and were without any weapons the whole time, they laid their Spears down on the sand between the women and the place they met us at; when we left them and rowing towards the point where the women were they got out of the Canoes and ran into the woods, the Men followed us along the shore.[77]

Governor Phillip himself visited on 9 March, on the way back from Botany Bay, and saw several Aborigines. It may be the same visit in which William Bradley records evidence:

> Landed in a Cove above Spring Cove and in Camp Cove, in which last we saw several of the Natives who ran away all but two, those stayed on the beach and one of them showed us the marks on his body where he had been beat and also cut on the shoulder by the people who landed here from two Boats, He made signs to us that the barbed spear had been jabbed several times into his shoulder: about 6. returned to the Ship.[78]

This same episode is recorded by Collins:

> There was, however, too much reason to believe that our people had been the aggressors, as the governor on his return from his excursion to Broken Bay, on landing at Camp Cove, found the natives there who had before frequently come up to him with confidence, unusually shy, and seemingly afraid of him and his party; and one, who after much invitation did venture to approach, pointed to some marks upon his shoulders, making signs they were caused by blows given with a stick. This, and their running away, whereas they had always before remained on the beach until the people landed from the boats, were strong indications that the man had been beaten by some of our stragglers. Eleven canoes full of people passed very near the Sirius, which was moored without the two points of the cove, but paddled away very fast upon the approach of some boats toward them.[79]

Bradley returned on 24 May 1788 to South Head — this time probably Inner South Head at the harbour entrance – where he recorded:

> Went to the South Head, observed the Latitude 33º:50':43' South and Captain Hunter 33º:51':07' South. Saw several Women fishing in Canoes without the

Head, they noticed us immediately and made a great noise, we threw them a handkerchief over the precipice which we saw them take up and throw by in one end of the Canoe.[80]

Worgan accompanied Hunter and Bradley on this trip where he recorded 5 or 6 women in canoes as well as (male) natives 'at a distance in the woods'.[81]

On 14 July Bradley visited Camp Cove and found the large fishing party had departed; he reported:

> On our return we went into Camp Cove where we found a Man & two children who appear'd to be starving we gave them Salt Beef which eagerly took & eat immediately, whilst the boats remained in the Cove, the Man went into the woods & brought in a root which he roasted, beat it with a stone which he frequently wet with a stone his mouth & when it was properly prepared he gave it to the Children to eat, the Man had many sores about him & was really a miserable object, the Boy & Girl appear'd to be about 5 or 6 years of age, the Boys teeth were complete as were the Girls fingers. We saw several Women fishing near the Cove but they would not land; we had two Seins with us, both of which were hauled several times without one fish being taken, some Birds were shot, all of which were given to the Old Man & his Children.[82]

Mobility was significant. Phillip noted:

> The winter months, in which fish is very scarce upon the coast, are June, July, August, and part of September. From the beaten paths that are seen between Port Jackson and Broken Bay, and in other parts, it is thought that the natives frequently change their situation, but it has not been perceived that they make any regular migrations to the northward in the winter months, or to the south in summer.[83]

A reconstruction of Aboriginal paths in the Sydney region notes (unreferenced) a track from North Bondi to Sydney Harbour near Vaucluse as well as the more substantial route from Botany Bay to the harbour east of Sydney.[84] The source is probably William Bradley who on 8 July 1788 found a good track from Rose Bay to Bondi Beach:

> Went down to one of the lower Coves and walked over to the Sand Hills which are given as a mark for a Ship coming from the Southward to know when they are near to Port Jackson, We found a good path over the neck of land, and not half an hour's walk.[85]

Val Attenbrow's comprehensive study of Aboriginal Sydney[86] notes place names recorded by colonists and visitors. The name of Gadigal or Cadigal people is associated with the area from South Head to Sydney Cove.[87] Phillip recorded in February 1790:

> From the entrance of the harbour, along the south shore, to the cover adjoining this settlement [i.e. Sydney] the district is called CADI, and the tribe CADIGAL, the women CADIGALLEON.[88]

Watkin Tench[89] defined the Cadigal as those who reside in the bay of Cadi. There is a possible link to the place name Kutti, which is probably Watsons Bay itself.[90]

Occupation and use changed with the advent of white settlement and the depopulation that followed this and the smallpox epidemic of 1790. But it is reasonable to assume some continuity of indigenous place names, while considering the earliest records to be the most reliable.[91]

Daniel Southwell, while based at the Signal Station at (Outer) South Head, recorded the name Woo-la-ra for where he was based ('The lookout'), Burra-wa-ra for Inner South Head, Mit-ta-la for Green Point (Laing's Point) and Ba-rab-ba-ra for 'the Mid-Rock' – Sow and Pigs Reef.[92] A manuscript vocabulary from 1790-2[93] confirms Metallar for Laing's Point (later also called Kubungarra), Birrabirra for Sow and Pigs reef, Barraory for Inner South Head, and gives the name Tarralbe for Outer South Head (near the Macquarie Lighthouse) as well as Pannerong for Rose Bay. There are later confirmations for the continuity of some of these names. And it to the later sources that we derive other Aboriginal names; Larmer[94] in 1832 recording Kutti for Watsons Bay beach. Moring for Vaucluse Point (Bottle and Glass Point) and Burrowwo for Steele or Shark Point south of Vaucluse – all confirmed by Mitchell about 1848.[95]

An Aboriginal informant, Nanbarry[96], made an unsubstantiated claim in 1790 to Daniel Southwell, then in charge of the new Signal Station established at (Outer) South Head, above Watsons Bay. He said this area was 'famed for its great engagements' and here were the graves of the dead. An apparent mock battle of 200 men had been seen near the harbour mouth on the north shore:

> The sailors who waited on the beach to take care of the boat saw about two hundred men assembled in two parties, who after some time drew themselves up on opposite sides, and from each party men advanced singly and threw their spears, guarding themselves at the same time with their shields. This seemed at first to be merely a kind of exercise, for the women belonging to both parties remained together on the beach; afterwards it had a more serious aspect, and the women are said to have run up and down in great agitation uttering violent shrieks. But it was not perceived that any men were killed.[97]

The area may be that closer to today's Signal Station and Macquarie Lighthouse, or may be referring to a much broader area of the peninsular, yet little evidence of grave use has been found. But the boy was young and may not be a reliable historical witness.[98]

The smallpox outbreak of 1790 was a definitive break in Aboriginal settlement of South Head. Half a century later it was an Aboriginal figure from northern Sydney, not from the Cadigal, who was found in the area. This information was from a visit around 1844 to Camp Cove by G.F. Angas with W.A. Miles. They recorded:

> about a dozen natives of the Sydney and Broken Bay tribes were encamped among the bushes on the margin of a small fresh-water lake close to Camp Cove.[99]

Here they met 'Queen Gooseberry' widow of a leading Aboriginal of the time of the first fleet, Bungaree.[100] This 'lake' – sometimes called the Duck Pond or the Wild Duck Pool[101] – was formed by a spring at the location which now forms a small park in the heart of Watsons Bay village between Camp Street and Cove Street. Angas also describes:

> natives spearing fish by torch-light, in the sheltered bays around Camp Cove, and in Camp Cove itself. They wade into the water until about knee deep, each man brandishing a flaming torch. Made of inflammable bark; this attracts the fish, and with their four-pronged spears they strike them with wonderful dexterity.[102]

Queen (Cora) Gooseberry was a familiar figure in colonial Sydney itself.[103] She died a few years later and is buried in Botany.

> Bungaree's wife, Cora Gooseberry, was known as 'Queen of Sydney to South Head' or 'Queen of Sydney and Botany' and was a Sydney identity for 20 years after Bungaree's death. Cora was often seen wrapped in a government issued blanket, her head covered with a scarf and a clay pipe in her mouth, sitting with her family and other Aborigines camped on the footpath outside the Cricketers' Arms, a hotel on the corner of Pitt and Market Streets in Sydney. She befriended the owner of the hotel Edward Borton who later owned the Sydney Arms Hotel in Castlereagh Street where he allowed Gooseberry to sleep at nights. Here she was eventually found dead at the age of 75, in July 1852 … At the time she was thought to be the last of the Kuring-gai clan to survive, but it later became evident that the descendants of the Kuring-gai people had joined remnants of other Aboriginal language groups to ensure their survival. Cora Gooseberry's gravestone is now in the Pioneers' cemetery at Botany.[104]

Thereafter Aboriginal life in the South Head peninsular appears minimally recorded. But there was still an Aboriginal group a little further southwest at Parsley Bay. William Francis Brown, who moved to Watsons Bay in 1892 aged 12, was to record 'When I was very young there was a blacks' camp at the head of the gully in Parsley Bay' and noted they would come to Watsons Bay on Sundays to demonstrate spear and boomerang throwing there in front of the Greenwich Pier Hotel (now Dunbar House).[105]

This brings Aboriginal settlement close to the 20th century.

Notes and References

1   Sources for geology: *1:100,000 sheet 9130 Sydney*, Sydney: Geological Survey of New South Wales, 1983; C. Herbert (ed.), *Geology of the Sydney 1:100,000 sheet 9130*, Sydney: Department of Mineral Resources, 1983.

2   T.O. O'Brien, 'Reminiscences of Bondi', *Journal of the Royal Australian Historical Society* 8, 1922: 362-5, p, 363

3   William Bradley, *A Voyage to New South Wales* [manuscript in State Library of New South Wales], 27 January 1788.

4   J.F. O'Connell & J. Allen, 'Dating the colonisation of Sahul (Pleistocene Australia – New Guinea): a review of recent research', *Journal of Archaeological Science* 31, 2004: 835-853.

5   V. Attenbrow, *Sydney's Aboriginal past: investigating the archaeological and historical record*, Sydney: University of New South Wales Press, 1992, pp. 37-9.

6   Herbert, *Geology*, p. 55: a medium to fine grained marine sand with podsol in the Dover Heights / Vaucluse area extending west from South Head General Cemetery.

7   *Soil Landscape Series sheet 9130, Sydney*, Sydney: Soil Conservation Service of NSW, 1989; G.A. Chapman & C.L. Murphy, *Soil landscapes of the Sydney 1:100,000 sheet*, Sydney: Soil Conservation Service of NSW, 1989.

8   http://www.nationalparks.nsw.gov.au/PDFs/EECinfo_Eastern_Suburbs_banksia_scrub.pdf

9   D.H. Benson & J. Howell, 'Taken for granted: the bushland of Sydney and its suburbs', Sydney: Kangaroo Press, 1990, pp. 25, 97-8; D.H. Benson & J. Howell, 'The natural vegetation of the Sydney 1:100,000 map sheet', *Cunninghamia* 3(4), 1994: 677-787, pp. 706-7.

10 A patch of similar geological origin carries this in North Head – map unit 21g in Benson & Howell 'Natural vegetation'.

11 Benson & Howell, 'Natural vegetation', pp. 701-2.

12 Benson & Howell, 'Taken for granted', pp. 23-5.

13 Benson & Howell, 'Taken for granted', pp. 99-100.

14 Attenbrow, *Sydney's Aboriginal past*, pp. 40-2.

15 R. Derricourt, 'The South Head peninsula of Sydney Harbour: boundaries in space and time', *Journal of the Royal Australian Historical Society* 96, 2010: 27-49.

16 National Parks and Wildlife Service Aboriginal Heritage Information Management System (hereafter NPWS) 45-6-2060.

17 O'Brien, 'Reminiscences of Bondi', p. 364.

18 NPWS 45-6-2169; R. Etheridge Junr. & T. Whitelegge, 'Aboriginal workshops on the coast of New South Wales, and their contents', *Records of the Australian Muse*um 6, 1907: 232-250; Plugshell, 'Aboriginal workshop at Bondi: tomahawks, grindstones, nose ornaments, etc.' *Eastern Suburbs Daily*, 12 September 1924 (copy at NPWS).

19 F.D. McCarthy, 'An analysis of the knapped implements from eight Elouera industry stations on the South Coast of New South Wales', *Records of the Australian Museum* 21, 1943: 127-153, especially pp. 145-149.

20 F.D. McCarthy, 'The Lapstone Creek excavation: two culture periods revealed in eastern New South Wales', *Records of the Australian Museum*, 22, 1948: 1-34.

21 Attenbrow, *Sydney's Aboriginal past*, pp. 155-7.

22 NPWS site 45-6-560; see V.J. Attenbrow & D. Steele, 'Fishing in Port Jackson, New South Wales – more than met the eye', *Antiquity* 69, 1995: 47-60; V.J. Attenbrow, *Port Jackson archaeological project: Stage II. Report on work carried out between January 1990 and 30 June 1992*, 1992 (MS: NPWS 2293); V.J. Attenbrow, *Port Jackson archaeological project: Stage II, Final report*, 1994 (MS: NPWS 2294).

23 Attenbrow & Steele, 'Fishing', pp. 57-8.

24 NPWS 45-6-2089.

25 Beth Rich, *Hermitage Foreshore reserve, Vaucluse: archaeological survey for Aboriginal sites along proposed walkway*, Sydney: NPWS, 1984 (MS: NPWS 768); T. Corkill, *Survey for Aboriginal archaeological sites at Strickland House, Vaucluse, N.S.W.*, Sydney: C. Haglund and Associates, 1990 (MS: NPWS 1888); NPWS sites 45-6-1628, 45-6-1629, 45-6-1651, 45-6-1652, 45-6-1627.

26 NPWS 45-6-1621.

27 NPWS 45-6-1761.

28 *Conservation Plan Nielsen Park Sydney Harbour National Park* Sydney: Department of Environment and Conservation (NSW) Parks & Wildlife Division, 2005, p 23.

29 NPWS site 45-6-1045; Attenbrow, *Port Jackson*.

30 NPWS 45-6-1044.

31 NPWS 45-6-0029.

32 NPWS 45-6-1469.

33 NPWS 45-6-2295.

34 NPWS 45-6-2172, 45-6-2174, 45-6-2175, 45-6-2176.

35 Recorded as NPWS 45-6-709 with a mention in WDC (see note 45 below).

36 NPWS 45-6-2084.

37 NPWS 45-6-96.

38 NPWS 45-6-1517.

39 *Daily Telegraph,* 28 August 1963, p. 5 (microfilm in State Library of NSW): then the front garden extending the home of Mr and Mrs Walter Phillips in Victoria Street.

40 'Many memories of Watsons Bay', *Wentworth Courier* 29 October 1986, p. 13 & p. 104; see also *An introduction to the Aboriginal history of the Woollahra Local Government Area,* Aboriginal History project Woollahra (Pamphlet in Woollahra Local History library), p. 15. A ground stone axe with Watsons Bay given as the provenance is in the Australian Museum collections, and has been placed on display in the Rocks Discovery Museum.

41 Australian Museum accession number E017714, on loan and display at the Rocks Discovery Museum in 2011; the museum holds correspondence reporting this find.

42 Australian Museum accession number E026981, also on loan and display at the Rocks Discovery Museum.

43 Australian Museum accession number E070707, found in 1929.

44 Australian Museum accession number E049114, catalogued in 1940.

45 W.D. Campbell, *Aboriginal Carvings of Port Jackson and Broken Bay, Sydney,* Memoirs of the Geological Survey of New South Wales, Ethnographical Series, 1, 1899, referred to below as WDC. A re-listing of these sites with topographical information and NPWS references is F.D. McCarthy (ed. E.A.K. Higginbotham) , *Catalogue of rock engravings in the Sydney – Hawkesbury district N.S.W.,* 2 vols., Sydney: National Parks and Wildlife Service, 1983.

46 NPWS 45-6-0691, WDC p. 9 pl. 2 fig. 4; NPWS 45-6-1690, NPWS 45-6-0734.

47 NPWS 45-6-0688; P. Stanbury & J. Clegg, *A field guide to Aboriginal rock engravings,* Sydney: Sydney University Press 1990, pp. 25-7; WDC pl. 2, fig. 12 & pl. 3, fig. 1; G.F. Angas, *Savage life and scenes in Australia and New Zealand,* 2 vols., London: Smith Elder, 1847, pp. 274-5, pl. 2; W.A. Miles, 'How did the natives of Australia become acquainted with the demigods and daemonia', *Journal of the Ethnological Society of London,* 3, 1854: 4-50, p. 32.

48 *Sydney Morning Herald,* 1 March 1986.

49 NPWS 45-6-903.

50 NPWS 45-6-1330; R. Griffin, 'Graven images on the Wentworth Estate', *Insites* (Sydney: Historic Houses Trust), Autumn 2006, pp. 6-7, David Lambert, *Report on rock art conservation and recording at Vaucluse House,* February 2005 (manuscript).

51 NPWS 45-6-704, WDC pl. 1, fig. 7.

52 NPWS 45-6-0711, 0713 and 0717; WDC pl. 1, fig. 8, 9 & 10.

53 NPWS 45-6-750; Attenbrow, Sydney's *Aboriginal pa*st, pp. 170-1.

54 NPWS 45-6-0720, Attenbrow, *Sydney's Aboriginal past* p. 171, WDC pl. 2, fig. 5.

55 NPWS 45-6-0719, Attenbrow. *Sydney's Aboriginal past,* pp. 168-171; WDC pl. 4, fig. 1-2.

56 NPWS 45-6-718, WDC pl. 2 fig. 13.

57 NPWS 45-6-1515.

58 Listed by Tia Negerevich, *Aboriginal Rock Engravings – South Head, Sydney Harbour. A report to the Australian department of Housing and Construction.* MS 1978 (NPWS archive).See also Margrit Koettig, *Assessment of Aboriginal sites in the area of HMAS Watson, South Head, Sydney, New South Wales,* Report MS 1986 (NPWS archive). These sites are given letters and many were in Campbell's survey volume (WDC) as follows:

    NPWS 45-6-713, WDC pl 2, fig 3, site F – wallaby or kangaroo
    NPWS 45-6-714, WDC pl. 2, fig. 2, site H – fishes
    NPWS 45-6-715, WDC pl. 1 fig. 1, site E – fishes, whale, wallaby, grooves
    NPWS 45-6-716, WDC pl. 2, fig. 1, site C – shark, stingray, fishes,, semicircle
    NPWS 45-6-723, WDC pl 1 fig. 6, site M – shark, fish, bandicoot, kangaroo, wallabies
    NPWS 45-6-724, WDC pl. 1, fig .5, site L - fish
    NPWS 45-6-733, WDC pl. 1 fig. 4, site B - humans
    NPWS 45-6-918, near WDC pl 1 fig 2, site S – fish, heart
    NPWS 45-6-919, WDC pl. 1 fig. 3, site K - swordfish
    NPWS 45-6-921, site A – fish, humans; in Angas, *Savage life,* vol. 2, pp. 274-5.
    NPWS 45-6-922, site D - fish

A site G (Negerevich) of pitted holes may be modern; site T (Koettig) is a possible marine animal.

59 *Historical Records of New South Wales* [*HRNSW*], Vol. 1, Part 2, p. 153; cf. A. Phillip, *The Voyage of Governor Phillip to Botany Bay,* London: Stockdale, 1793, entry for 22 April 1788.

60 W. Tench, *Sydney's first four years,* ed. LF Fitzhardinge, 1979, Sydney: Library of Australian History, p. 47.

61 By C.A. Leseur, redrawn and reproduced in François Peron, *Voyage de découvertes aux terres Australes,* Paris:

Arthus Bertrand, 1824, pl. 33.

62 BP = before present, i.e. before 1950 as measured by radiocarbon dating.

63 J. Mulvaney & J. Kamminga, *Prehistory of Australia*, Sydney: Allen & Unwin, 1999, pp. 230-234.

64 Mulvaney, *Prehistory*, p. 274.

65 J. Kohen, *Aboriginal environmental impacts*, Sydney: UNSW Press, 1995, pp. 81-2.

66 Attenbrow, *Sydney's Aboriginal past*, pp. 156-8.

67 Kohen, *Aboriginal environmental impacts*, pp. 80-1.

68 P.G. Fidlon (ed.), *The Journal and Letters of Lt. Ralph Clark, 1787-1792*, Sydney: Australian Documents Library, 1981, p. 93.

69 Daniel Southwell papers in *HRNSW* vol. 3, p. 663.

70 *HRNSW* vol. 1.2, p. 309.

71 Governor Phillip to Lord Sydney, 9 July 1788. *HRNSW*, Vol. 1, Part 2, p. 153.

72 *HRNSW* vol 1.2, pp. 148-9; on p. 167 it is called a small cove, and Bronte seems a very possible location.

73 A. Phillip, *The Voyage of Governor Phillip to Botany Bay* [1789], Sydney: Angus & Robertson, 1970, pp. 63-4.

74 Phillip, *Voyage*, 9 July 1788.

75 *HRNSW* vol. 1.2, p 191; Phillip, *Voyage*, 9 July 1788.

76 J. Cobley, *Sydney Cove 1788*, Sydney: Hodder, 1962.

77 William Bradley, *A Voyage to New South Wales, December 1786 - May 1792*, [Journal in State Library of New South Wales], 28 January 1788.

78 Though dated 10 March: Bradley, *Voyage*, 10 March 1788.

79 D. Collins, *An account of the English Colony in New South Wales [1798]*, vol. 1, Christchurch: Whitcombe & Tombs, 1910, p. 25.

80 Bradley, *Voyage*, 24 May 1788.

81 G.B. Worgan, *Journal of a First Fleet Surgeon*, Sydney: Library of Australian History, 1978, pp. 46-7.

82 Bradley, *Voyage*, 14 July 1788.

83 Phillip, *Voyage*, 9 July 1788.

84 G. Aplin (ed.), *A difficult infant*, Sydney: NSW University Press, 1988, fig. 2.3: source not given.

85 Bradley, *Voyage*, 8 July 1788.

86 Attenbrow, *Sydney's Aboriginal past*, pp. 9-13.

87 Attenbrow, *Sydney's Aboriginal past*, pp. 24-5.

88 *HRNSW*, vol. 1.2. p. 309 (A. Phillip, 13 February 1790).

89 Tench, *Sydney's First Four Years*, p. 292.

90 The 2006 exhibition at the New South Wales State Library made the claim that the probable heartland of the Cadigal was Camp Cove – but there is no supporting evidence for such a claim. It also noted that Cadi (gadi) was the word for the Xanthorrhoea grass trees in the area. See *Eora: mapping Aboriginal Sydney*, p. 4 at http://www.sl.nsw.gov.au/events/exhibitions/2006/eora/docs/eora-guide.pdf

91 A full collation of place names appears in Attenbrow, *Sydney's Aboriginal past*, pp. 9-13.

92 *HRNSW*, vol. 3, p. 699.

93 'Vocabulary of the language of N.S. Wales in the neighbourhood of Sydney', MS 41645, School of Oriental and African Studies, London [copy in Mitchell Library]; reference from Attenbrow, *Sydney's Aboriginal past*.

94 J. Larmer, 'Native names of points of land in Port Jackson' [1832], *Journal of the Royal Society of NSW*, 32, 1898), pp. 223-229.

95 T.L. Mitchell, 'Native names of points and islands in Port Jackson', manuscript in Mitchell Library, reference from Attenbrow, *Sydney's Aboriginal past*.

96 Nanbarry was a nephew of the Cadigal elder Colebee, and accompanied Bennelong on sea voyages with the British. A pencil drawing of him by Thomas Watling is in the Natural History Museum, London.

97 Phillip, *Voyages*, 9 July 1788.

98 'The surgeon general has had a fine boy with him these two years called Nanbarry, he speaks pretty good English but is too young to give any information and it is probable will forget his native tongue' Mitchell Library, MLMSS 6937/1/1, 12 August 1790.

99 Angas, *Savage life*, vol. 2, p. 202.

100 Angas, *Savage life*, vol. 2, p. 273.

101 J. Jervis (ed. V. Kelly), *The History of Woollahra*, Sydney: Municipal Council of Woollahra [n.d. 1960], p. 10.

102 Angas, *Savage life*, vol. 2, p. 200.

103 A portrait by Charles Rodius from 1844 is in the Mitchell Library *(SSV* SP Coll Rodius 12,)*, and another by the same artist (SV*/Sp Coll/Rodius/3), as is her breastplate (R 251b). Another portrait was published in the 1840s: see National Library of Australia nla.pic-an8953993; Angas' watercolour 'Old Queen Gooseberry, widow of Bungaree', Sydney 1848, is in the South Australian Museum AA8/4/2/1.

104 http://www.cityofsydney.nsw.gov.au/Barani/themes/print/theme7_p.htm

105 W.F. Brown, 'Many memories of Watsons Bay', *Wentworth Courier*, 29 October 1986, p. 13 & p. 104.

2

Colonial Government and South Head

The groups of Cadigal who were on the South Head peninsula on 7 May 1770[1] experienced something hitherto unparalleled: the site of a European sailing ship, the *Endeavour*, travelling northwards off the coast of their fishing territory. Eighteen years later this vision was to turn into a transformation of everything.

First European settlement

South Head and the adjacent settlement which would be called Watson's Bay (now spelled Watsons Bay) played a major part in the early history of New South Wales, from the very beginning of the colony in 1788 through the 68 years to self-government in 1855-6, and beyond. South Head marked the entrance to the harbour, Port Jackson, in which lay the centre of the new colony, Sydney Cove. Here, through the establishment of its lookout, flagstaff, signal station, pilot base and lighthouses, lay keys to the colony's link with the outside world.

One of the ironies of Australian history is that Captain James Cook exulted in the importance of Botany Bay, but passed by the entrance to Port Jackson with little comment, though leaving a brief record to alert the next European arrivals.

Cook sailed north from his long anchorage in Botany Bay, to continue his major voyage of exploration. Cook's log made no formal record of Port Jackson, though it and the heads were marked on his charts. But in the Admiralty Journal kept by Cook it is recorded that he came:

> abreast of a Bay or Harbour wherein there appeared to be safe anchorage which I called Port Jackson. It lies 3 leagues to the northward of Botany Bay.[2]

But he did not pause and he continued northward.

Six years later the American War of Independence broke out and after losing their American colonies in 1783, the British government had to consider alternative locations for despatching long term criminal prisoners. Following the urging of James Matra and

Joseph Banks, who had been on Cook's 1770 expedition, what we now call the First Fleet left England under the command of Captain Arthur Phillip in May 1787 and arrived in Botany Bay from 18 January 1788. This area's limitations for a sustainable economy were soon visible and on 22 January[3] Phillip and a small group in three small 'barges' sailed north to investigate the potential of the briefly mentioned Port Jackson.

They were observed by Aboriginal people from the cliffs between Botany Bay and South Head:

> The governor set off on Monday the 21st, accompanied by Captain Hunter, Captain Collins (the judge-advocate), a lieutenant, and the master of the Sirius, with a small party of marines for their protection, the whole being embarked in three open boats. The day was mild and serene, and there being but a gentle swell without the mouth of the harbour, the excursion promised to be a pleasant one. Their little fleet attracted the attention of several parties of the natives, as they proceeded along the coast, who all greeted them in the same words, and in the same tone of vociferation, shouting every where 'Warra, warra, warra', words which, by the gestures that accompanied them, could not be interpreted into invitations to land, or expressions of welcome.[4]

The exploration was later described by Jacob Nagle, a seaman with the group whose account – with spelling and punctuation here corrected and modernised – brings South Head into the European world. When writing this he could use the place names which were given by the early colony:

> The Governor wished to see Port Jackson before any improvement was made in Botany Bay. Three boats were got ready with three days' provisions to go round to Port Jackson, a number of officers and some marines. In the morning we started, it being about five leagues by water, but we found afterwards it was not more than 5 or 6 miles across by land. We arrived in the afternoon and ran up Middle Harbour to the westward, and then a circular round to a bay on the north side, which Governor Phillip called Manly Bay, and surveyed round till we came into the SW branch.[5]

Phillip noted of the Aborigines in this area that 'several women landed from their canoes the morning the boat stopped in a small bay near the entrance of the harbour, when I was going to examine the coast to the northwest'.[6] Nagle's narrative continues:

> Coming in to the heads of the harbour on the north side is a high cliff of rocks, and on the south side a low point, but rocks, and abreast the harbour's mouth on the opposite side of the harbour is a high cliff of rocks and flat on the top. It coming on dark, we landed on a beach on the south side and there pitched our tents for the night. This was called Camp Cove. The marines were put on their posts. The sailors were variously employed, some kindling fires and some shooting the seine [net] for fish, others getting out utensils for cooking. By the time we got our suppers, was late in the night, and by four in the morning we had everything in the boats again, and on our oars, with one man at the lead sounding out of

one cove into the other, Capt. Hunter, Mr. Bradley [*sic*], and the master taking a draught of the soundings, likewise the distances. We ate our breakfasts on our seats and pulled all day.[7]

The error in including Bradley on this voyage, in a narrative written down long after the events, may throw some doubt on detail but the story of the camp – giving its origin to the name Camp Cove – sounds realistic and is taken to imply the first landfall by Europeans within Port Jackson.[8] With arrival in the dark and departure before dawn, there would have been no opportunity to explore the hinterland. Camp Cove had a freshwater spring behind the beach so proved a suitable place for a night's camp. The next day Nagle successfully fished while Phillip and his party went ashore at what was to be named Sydney Cove (the future Circular Quay), the centre of the new settlement.

Phillip's party returned to Botany Bay, gave out the good news about the suitability for settlement of Port Jackson and especially Sydney Cove, and the whole fleet moved on 26 January 1788 to the new site. A painting made by Lieutenant William Bradley recreates the scene of the fleet passing through the Heads,[9] and another drawn from North Head recreates the image of the Supply passing by South Head.[10]

The Supply entering Port Jackson 1788, watched from Aboriginal canoes
SOURCE 'View in Port Jackson from the South Head leading up to Sydney ; Supply sailing in', William Bradley - Drawings from his journal 'A Voyage to New South Wales', Mitchell Library, State Library of NSW, Call number: Safe 1 / 14, Folio 17.

The first months of European settlement at Sydney Cove saw many excursions of exploration around the Harbour and its bays. Captain John Hunter led a party which returned to Camp Cove just two days after the first European settlement at Sydney Cove, this time encountering Aboriginal people fishing, and further visits are recorded by Phillip on 9 March and by Bradley on 1 July and again on 14 July 1798.

Travel by horse was not an option – only seven horses landed with the First Fleet – and exploration by foot could be dangerous, as shown by clashes between Aborigines and

Europeans, thus requiring an armed guard for any trip away from the settlement. However exploration by boat was relatively safe and allowed the senior officers of the colony to familiarise themselves with the bays of Port Jackson. It was not only the senior officials who travelled around the harbour. Jacob Nagle, who had recorded the first European landfall in Port Jackson, would return to fish between the town and the harbour mouth, though at least some of this was up Middle Harbour:

> Our customary method was to leave Sydney Cove about four o'clock in the afternoon and go down the harbour and fish all night from one cove to another. We would then make a fire on the beach, cook our supper, and take our grog, lay down in the sand before the fire, wet or dry, and go to sleep till morning, though we would be often disturbed by the natives heaving their spears at us at a distance, and being in the night, it would be by random. In the morning we would return, taking the fish to the Governor's house, where they would be shared out, as far as they would go.[11]

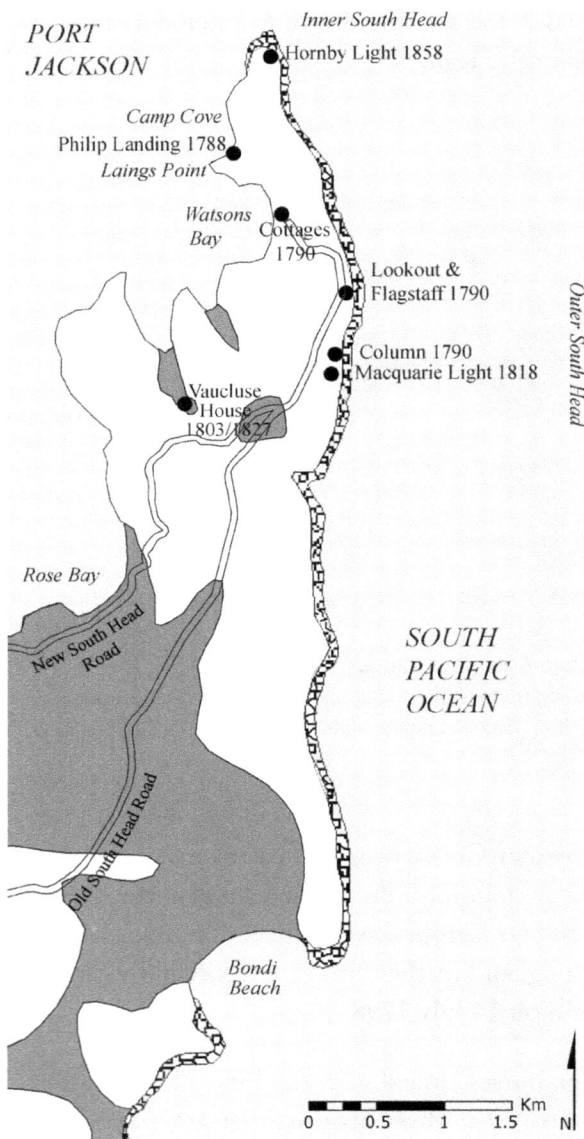

Settlement and early colonial activity on the South Head peninsula
SOURCE Derricourt, 'The South Head peninsula'

The shelter afforded by Camp Cove, and the nearby beach which was to become Watsons Bay, also made it a suitable place to anchor overnight before an early start out through the Heads. Bradley and others camped there on 26 August 1789 before departing to survey Broken Bay,[12] and a Dutch ship anchored at what by then could be called 'the lookout cove' on 3 February 1791.[13] Three convicts managed to reach this ship to try and board it and escape, but were apprehended.

The land became safer for Europeans after the impact on the Aboriginal community caused by the smallpox outbreak, observed from as early as April and May 1789.[14] The substantial reduction of the Cadigal community was noted widely. When Bradley visited (Outer) South Head on 29

January 1790 he made a note of sighting black kangaroo, which might imply the absence of Aboriginal hunters.[15] Subsequent Aboriginal visits seem to be by those who had become familiar with the European town and familiar to its residents.

Thus over two years South Head moved from a place of intensive Aboriginal fishing, to a place of periodic visits by the Europeans, until on 20 January 1790 it became the site of a major and lasting initiative, as a lookout and signal station, on the initiative of Captain Hunter.

Lookout

The colony was desperate for the arrival of supplies from an expected second fleet, but such a support expedition would be travelling to Botany Bay, and would not know of the removal of settlement to Port Jackson. Therefore each week for the first eighteen months of settlement, a party of marines was sent overland to Botany Bay to see if any vessel had arrived there.[16] Hunter's idea, put into effect some twelve days after the *Supply* left for Norfolk Island with convicts and provisions, was for a lookout at Outer South Head, which would be a better use of resources. From here a permanent guard would watch out for arriving ships, raising a flag both to give them a sign of the new location of the settlement, and to notify the colony of the imminent arrival of the long awaited ships. Once instituted the mechanism became the continuing basis for information on arriving vessels. Hunter explained:

> We landed in this country with two years provisions, at least with what was supposed, when we sailed from England, would be the case; that time was now elapsed, yet we had not been visited by any ships from Europe, and we still had remaining provisions, at half allowance, to last until June. We all looked forward with hope for arrivals with a relief; and that every assistance necessary for strangers might be at hand, I offered, with a few men from the Sirius, to go down to the south head of the harbour, there to build a lookout-house, and erect a flag-staff upon the height, which might be seen from the sea; and which might also communicate information of ships in the offing to the governor at Sydney-cove. The governor approved my proposals. I went down with six men, and was accompanied by Mr. White and Mr. Worgan, the surgeons of the settlement and Sirius. We erected a flag-staff, and lived in a tent for ten days, in which time we completed a tolerably good house. At the end of ten days, I was relieved by Mr. Bradley with a fresh party.[17]

Watkin Tench tells a similar story:

> For eighteen months after we had landed in the country, a party of marines used to go weekly to Botany Bay, to see whether any vessel, ignorant of our removal to Port Jackson, might be arrived there. But a better plan was now devised, on the suggestion of Captain Hunter. A party of seamen were fixed on a high bluff, called the South-head, at the entrance of the harbour, on which a flag was ordered to be

hoisted, whenever a ship might appear, which should serve as a direction to her, and as a signal of approach to us. Every officer stepped forward to volunteer a service which promised to be so replete with beneficial consequences. But the zeal and alacrity of Captain Hunter, and our brethren of the 'Sirius', rendered superfluous all assistance or co-operation. Here on the summit of the hill, every morning from daylight until the sun sunk, did we sweep the horizon, in hope of seeing a sail.[18]

The flagstaff was visible from the higher land bordering Sydney Cove – the east side where the government farm was sited, and especially the west side which we now call Observatory Hill above The Rocks.[19] The location chosen had to be high enough to be seen from Sydney, and as far east as possible to gain the maximum sight lines to and from the sea to the south, past and over the point of Ben Buckler north of Bondi Beach.[20]

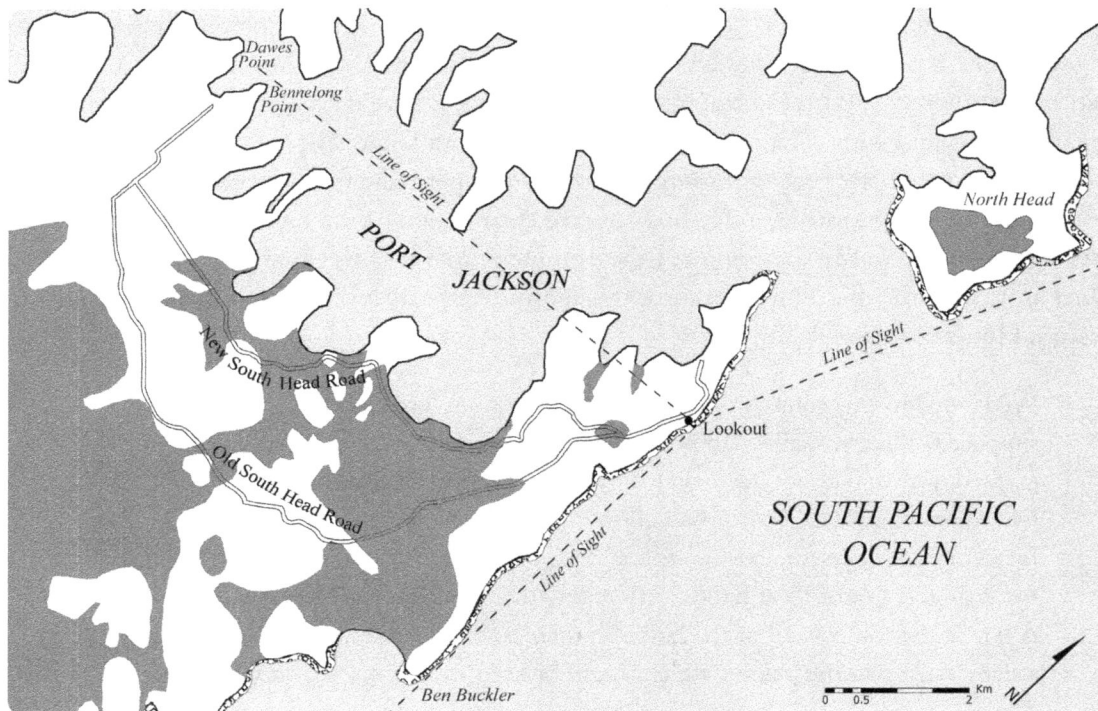

Lines of sight from the Lookout
SOURCE Derricourt, 'South Head Peninsula'

Within these constraints, the site chosen also needed to be close enough to the landing place in today's Watsons Bay to allow the transport of building materials, foodstuffs and personnel, all brought by water. The location that best meets these criteria is that marked by today's Signal Station and the adjacent flagstaff at Dunbar Head. In reality no ship entering Botany Bay from close to shore in the South could see such a signal flag - a ship would need to be about 3.5 km or almost 2 nautical miles east of the bay entrance to see past Ben Buckler. But from Dunbar Head the sightline goes over the extremity of Ben Buckler head, so a ship one kilometre closer to shore could still be seen by the Lookout. Spotting the flagstaff from such a distance at sea would be more challenging - but any vessel would be seen and would subsequently see the flagstaff after finding Botany Bay unoccupied and sailing on.

It has been suggested the location may have been further south on the highest ground (occupied by the later lighthouse)[21] but that gives only slightly greater visibility from sea for a significantly further distance from the harbour landing site. The flagstaff is shown with the flag flying in a coastal view by George Raper from 1790.[22]

Flagstaff at Outer South Head 1790
SOURCE George Raper, 'Views of land in the neighbourhood of Port Jackson', drawing, Natural History Museum London

Bradley took over command at the Lookout on 29ᵗ January, and five days later on 3 February Governor Phillip paid a visit of inspection, accompanied by the Aboriginal Benelong, who impressed Bradley by throwing a spear 98 yards against the wind. On their return to Sydney, Benelong recognised Aboriginal women on a point near Rose Bay.[23]

Bradley seems to have still been at the Lookout on 7 February while the young Aboriginal Nanbarry (Nanbaray) visited,[24] and demonstrated the local method of starting a fire (as well as the traditional method of digging a grave).[25]

And the Lookout came into its own just three days later when the *Supply* was sighted, on return from Norfolk Island, briefly raising false expectations in the colony:

> The first signal from the flagstaff at the South Head was displayed on the 10th of February; and though every imagination first turned toward the expected stranger, yet happening about the time at which the Supply was expected from Norfolk Island, conjecture soon fixed on the right object; and the temporary suspense was put an end to, by word being brought up to the settlement, that the Supply, unable to get into Port Jackson, had borne up for Botany Bay, in which harbour she anchored in the dusk of the evening.[26]

But at least the first test of the flagstaff idea showed the colony that it worked!

The Lookout required permanent manning, and Lieutenant Bradley could hardly be spared permanently for such a supervisory role.

The *Sirius* was prepared for a trip to China to secure supplies, but then the plan was changed to visit Norfolk Island before returning to undertake the further voyage. It was decided that one the Master's Mates of the *Sirius* could be spared take over the command at the Lookout and Bradley – no doubt with some relief – noted that the Governor arrived at the end of February with his relief and a support crew of six.[27]

The reluctant new appointee was Daniel Southwell, who had been a Midshipman on the *Sirius*, and whose journal as well as letters home to England gives us a fuller view of the first European settlement at South Head.[28] With regret he watched while the *Supply* and his own ship the *Sirius* sailed north on 6 March, longing for its return so he could resume his naval duties. But it never did return for it was wrecked two weeks later on the reef at Norfolk Island. The return of the *Supply* on her own was marked by the raising of the flag at the Flagstaff. Tench wrote:

> To satisfy myself that the flag was really flying, I went to the observatory, and looked for it through the large astronomical telescope, when I plainly saw it. But I was immediately convinced that it was not to announce the arrival of ships from England; for I could see nobody near the flagstaff except one solitary being, who kept strolling around, unmoved by what he saw. I well knew how different an effect the sight of strange ships would produce.[29]

Southwell's writings give a clearer view of the arrangements at South Head. There were up to eleven men stationed there, though only eight in July, including his companion Harris. They took turns in four hour shifts throughout all hours of daylight to watch for shipping, living further down the slope 'about a mile away' (in reality less) by what was later called Watsons Bay[30] 'where are the houses, or rather whitewashed cottages, in a valley adjoining to the garden, and near the beach. … We have a rill of fresh water at a stone's throw on each hand.'[31]

By April they had started a garden:

> the ground is tolerably good, and we are now and then supplied with a few greens from a garden that was intended for the ship's use. A boat is also allowed us, and we have good opportunities to try our luck at fishing. There are likewise musquets and ammunition for the defence of the place, and the situation, through so retired, has its advantages.[32]

And by July he could report:

> Our infant garden at this place exhibits a pleasing prospect of vegetation. Seven or eight thousand head of green, and daily planting some bed of turnip, radish &c, have rewarded our little labour.[33]

Elizabeth Macarthur's correspondence reflects a more relaxed life of a pioneer; she arrived in Sydney aged 22 in 1790. In a letter home in March 1791 she described a visit to South Head:

> We passed the day in walking among the Rocks, and upon the sands very agreeable. I looked carefully for some Shells for you, but could find none better than what you can get at Bude or Widemouth. Above this Bay, about half a mile's

distance, is a very high Hill which commands an extensive view of the Wide Ocean. On it is placed a Flag-Staff, which can also be seen at Sydney. When a ship appears the Flag is hoisted, by which means we have notice of it much sooner than we otherways could have; it also conducts the vessel into the Harbour. There are a few huts near the Flag-Staff, with People in them appointed to keep a look-out, and from thence the spot has derived the general name of Look-out. [34]

The charm of the situation was greater for visitors than for those stationed there. On 23 July 1791, William Norris and William Roberts, privates in the marines, were sent there effectively as a punishment. They were associated with a burglary of liquor and other items; though they were found not guilty the suspicion remained and they were assigned to duty at the Lookout: 'it was judged necessary to place them where they would be disabled from concerting any future scheme' with the supposed ringleader.[35]

One boat, when available, had to serve the whole group, and convey additional personnel, food and supplies to the Lookout crew and messages and personnel back to Sydney Cove. The boat was in use elsewhere when, in July 1790, Southwell and one of his crew went to Sydney by foot following close to the shore, meeting in Rose Bay with a group of Aborigines, with their canoes, spears and fishing tackle.[36]

The boat journey, usually safe, was the setting for a tragedy in the same month. Two of Southwell's crew were 17 year old James Ferguson and marine James Bates (whose posting to South Head seems to have been by way of punishment). On 23 July they took a flat bottomed boat with two visiting marines, when near Bradley's Point a whale rose from the harbour and sank the vessel. Only one of the marines managed to reach the shore at Rose Bay and make his way back up to the Lookout, waiting there until another boat came the next day to investigate what had happened. Southwell himself was visiting Sydney Cove at this time.[37] Subsequently,

> The body of one of the unfortunate people who were drowned at the latter end of July last with Mr. Ferguson was found about the close of this month, washed on shore in Rose Bay, and very much disfigured. The whale which occasioned this accident, we were informed, had never found its way out of the harbour, but, getting on shore in Manly Bay, was killed by the natives, and was the cause of numbers of them being at this time assembled to partake of the repasts which it afforded them [see below].[38]

The purpose for which the Lookout was established was fulfilled on 3 June 1790 with the sighting of the *Lady Juliana*, the first vessel of the Second Fleet. The flag was raised and Sydney settlement responded.

> At length the clouds of misfortune began to separate, and on the evening of the 3rd of June, the joyful cry of 'the flag's up' resounded in every direction.
>
> I was sitting in my hut, musing on our fate, when a confused clamour in the street drew my attention. I opened my door, and saw several women with children in their arms running to and fro with distracted looks, congratulating each other, and

kissing their infants with the most passionate and extravagant marks of fondness. I needed no more; but instantly started out, and ran to a hill, where, by the assistance of a pocket glass, my hopes were realized. My next door neighbour, a brother-officer, was with me, but we could not speak. We wrung each other by the hand, with eyes and hearts overflowing.

Finding that the governor intended to go immediately in his boat down the harbour, I begged to be of his party.

As we proceeded, the object of our hopes soon appeared: a large ship, with English colours flying, working in, between the heads which form the entrance of the harbour. The tumultuous state of our minds represented her in danger; and we were in agony. Soon after, the governor, having ascertained what she was, left us, and stepped into a fishing boat to return to Sydney. The weather was wet and tempestuous but the body is delicate only when the soul is at ease. We pushed through wind and rain, the anxiety of our sensations every moment redoubling. At last we read the word 'London' on her stern. 'Pull away, my lads! She is from Old England! A few strokes more, and we shall be aboard! Hurrah for a bellyful, and news from our friends!' Such were our exhortations to the boat's crew.

A few minutes completed our wishes, and we found ourselves on board the 'Lady Juliana' transport, with two hundred and twenty-five of our countrywomen whom crime or misfortune had condemned to exile.[39]

The signal was repeated on several days in June as the remainder of the Second Fleet arrived. Thereafter in private and public records, the arrival of a ship is noted by a phrase such as 'the signal was made at the South Head', 'the signal for a sail in the offing was flown at South Head'.

In August – perhaps in response to talking to the Second Fleet commander of their experience of arrival, Phillip wrote to England:

As ships coming in with the land do not readily discover the entrance of this harbour, a stone building will be erected in the course of a few weeks, very near the South Head, which will be sufficient mark for those who are not acquainted with the coast.[40]

The response was two years in coming:

The commander of ships hereafter to be despatched will be apprised of the landmark you have erected to direct their passage into Port Jackson, which, on a coast so little known, appears to have been a measure extremely necessary and proper.[41]

In 1790 stones were being cut ready for a column to be erected as a signal to shipping[42] 'to be built on the high land by the flagstaff'. According to Collins, 'the stonemasons were sent down to quarry stone upon the spot for the building'.[43] A plan showed the intention for it to be 4 feet by 4 feet on a platform raised six feet high, south of the Lookout shelter.

Sea   Coast

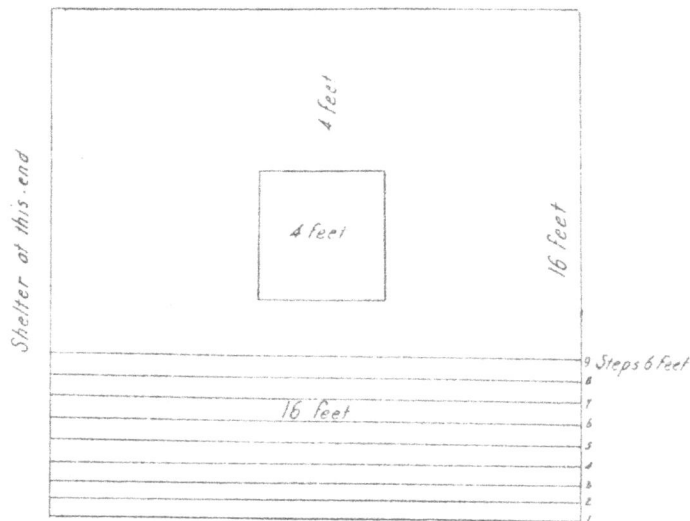

Shelter at this end

4 feet

4 feet

16 feet

16 feet

9 Steps 6 feet

Plan for the column by the Lookout constructed 1790
SOURCE enclosure in letter of Daniel Southwell to Revd W Butler, reproduced in HRNSW volume 2, p. 719

Governor Phillip had gone with Henry Waterhouse in September 1790 'to mark out a place to build a Column as a mark for ships coming from sea'.[44] Hunter records:

> In the morning of the 7th of September, Governor Phillip went down the harbour to fix on a spot for raising a brick column, which might point out the entrance to ships which were unacquainted with the coast, as the flag-staff could not be seen by vessels until they drew very near the land, and was also liable to be blown down … rising ground at the distance of a cable's length from the south head was chosen, and the stone necessary for the base of the column being already cut, that work was immediately begun.[45]

There was a dramatic development that same day. A whale, perhaps the one that had caused the tragedy in Port Jackson, was beached at Manly where it was being consumed in a large feast. Nanbarry and a group of men from the colony arrived and found Benelong among them, who on learning the Governor was nearby expressed the hope the Governor would visit.

He was about to return from South Head to Sydney Cove when his party was informed of the request. They went down[46] to collect muskets and other equipment from the Lookout and went across the Heads to Manly. But tension grew and one of the Aborigines threw a spear which penetrated Phillip's shoulder. He and his party escaped back to Sydney Cove.[47] Collins described the incident:

> The governor … went down in the morning of the 7th to the South Head, accompanied by Captain Collins and Lieutenant Waterhouse, to give some

instructions to the people employed in erecting a column at that place. As he was returning to the settlement, he received information … that Bennillong [Benelong] had been seen there by Mr. White, and had sent the governor as a present a piece of the whale which was then lying in the wash of the surf on the beach. Anxious to see him again, the governor, after taking some arms from the party at the Lookout, which he thought the more requisite in this visit as he heard the cove was full of natives, went down and landed at the place where the whale was lying. … The cove was full of natives allured by the attractions of a whale feast; and it being remarked during the conference that the twenty or thirty which appeared were drawing themselves into a circle round the governor and his small unarmed party … the governor proposed retiring to the boat by degrees; but Bennillong, who had presented to him several natives by name, pointed out one, whom the governor, thinking to take particular notice of, stepped forward to meet, holding out both his hands toward him. The savage not understanding this civility, and perhaps thinking that he was going to seize him as a prisoner, lifted a spear from the grass with his foot, and fixing it on his throwing-stick, in an instant darted it at the governor.[48]

Phillip returned to Sydney and recovered from the wound.

In mid January 1791 a misadventure of a different kind happened; as recorded by Hunter

About the middle of the month a theft of an extraordinary nature was committed by some of the natives. It had been the custom to leave the signal colours during the day at the flagstaff on the South Head, at which place they were seen by some of these people, who, watching their opportunity, ran away with them, and they were afterwards seen divided among them in their canoes, and used as coverings.[49]

Phillip visited the Lookout again on 26 November 1791, after seeing the *Supply* off to England.[50]

In May 1792 the European population at South Head was supplemented with the establishment of a fishery 'exclusively for the use of the sick: under a man named Barton who was also to act as a pilot for ships.[51]

On 20 June 1792 Collins reported

The flag-staff which had been erected at the South Head under the direction of Captain Hunter, in the month of January 1790, being found too short to show the signal at any great distance, a new one was taken down the harbour, and erected the day the Atlantic arrived, within a few feet of the other; its height above ground was sixty feet.[52]

The staff of the Lookout at South Head could usefully have looked inwards as well as outwards. In September 1790 convicts took a punt from Rose Hill (Parramatta) at night to South Head, stole the boat used by the Lookout crew, and rowed out to sea.

A hazardous enterprise (but when liberty is the stake, what enterprise is too hazardous for its attainment!) was undertaken in this month by five convicts at Rose Hill, who, in the night, seized a small punt there, and proceeded in her to the South Head, whence they seized and carried off a boat, appropriated to the use of the lookout house, and put to sea in her, doubtless with a view of reaching any port they could arrive at, and asserting their freedom. They had all come out in the last fleet; and for some time previous to their elopement, had been collecting fishing tackle, and hoarding up provisions, to enable them to put their scheme into execution.[53]

Another account comes from Hunter:

> In the night of the 26th of September, five convicts took a punt from Rose-Hill, in which they came down to the look-out, where they exchanged the punt for a four-oared boat, and got off undiscovered. These people certainly meant to go along the coast to the northward, and to attempt getting to some of the Friendly islands; but this project must be almost impossible, and there was every reason to suppose they would perish in a very few days.[54]

These were possibly the five convicts arrested in 1795 in Port Stephens. They were reported to have worked their way down the harbour, stolen a 'wretched weak boat' (at Watsons Bay) from the Lookout staff, and taken it out of the harbour where one met his death and the other four ('miserable, naked, dirty and smoke-dried') escaped to the north; to be recaptured at Port Stephens and brought back to the colony.[55]

A fire was lit each night at South Head, in a cauldron raised on a tripod, to warn ships.[56] In a storm in August 1795, the column built at South Head as a signal to shipping collapsed but was readily mended.[57] In the summer of 1796-97 another storm destroyed the flagstaff.[58]

In March 1805 a new flagstaff was raised 'considerably taller, and of course much more conspicuous and better adapted.'[59] Periodic repairs continued; In January 1827 it was noted that the signal post had been 'seriously indisposed from a fracture in one of the limbs at least these last three weeks' and the repairs took two months time to be completed, perhaps suggesting the importance of the signal had diminished.[60]

Violence of a different kind affected the Lookout a year after, when a soldier posted to the Lookout went missing, and his body was found two days later on Christmas Day 1797 in an abused state. A soldier with whom he had been arguing was suspected but nothing could be proved:

> On the morning of Christmas Day, the governor was informed that two seamen belonging to the Reliance had discovered the body of a soldier (who had been for two days missing from the look-out post on the South Head, where he was on duty), lying in a mangled state, the head and hands being cut off. Some words having passed between him and a soldier, who had been also heard to threaten him, he was suspected of having committed the murder, and on the 30th was put on his trial for the same. Nothing, however, appeared before the court that could

substantiate the charge of murder against him; neither was it clearly ascertained that violent hands had been laid on the deceased. As it had been foreseen that direct proof would be wanting, it was deemed expedient to obtain what might be, though not positive, yet of a nature to be nearly as satisfactory. With this view, the suspected person was directed to handle and bury the body, which he did without any apparent emotion; nor did the body bleed at his touch, or exhibit any sign that superstition or ignorance could turn into an accusation against him; he observing at the same time, that, as he had never had any quarrel with the deceased, he could have no objection to perform this last friendly office for him.[61]

There is a later mention of South Head in a criminal context. In 1800, under Governor King, a political plot of Irish nationalists was uncovered in which it was suggested that 'many of the soldiers would be ready to join and take the guns to South Head and other places of security'.[62]

The Lookout at South Head remained a stable operation at an appropriately small level. In Governor King's listing of the military establishment in 1804,[63] he lists six rank and file members of the New South Wales Corps as stationed at South Head. This would be enough to cover a daily roster of watch, to tend to the gardens that supported them and to journey into town for further supplies and for a change of personnel. King noted the battery on the other side of the harbour at George's Head, and suggested

> in order to fortify the harbour it would be necessary to have a battery of twelve eighteen-pounders on the inner South Head, one side to face the east[64] but it would be many years before such armaments were to be put in place.

Repairs continued to be needed to the flagstaff and signal station over the years.[65]

The flagstaff with the tapered column to the south – described as a "pyramid" or "obelisk" – is shown in the far distance of contemporary paintings of Sydney, which may not be reliable in detail.[66] A map of the colony, [67] published in 1802, from a draft in 1796[68] shows at Outer South Head a 'pyramid' to the south and the icon of a flagstaff to the north, by which is marked a 'Lookout' with a symbol for settlement just west of it, close to Watsons Bay itself. To the north is marked the land grant made to Edward Laing at Camp Cove. Copies were made of the map first surveyed by John Hunter in 1788, adding new names and detail: Green Point, Camp Cove and Rose Bay.[69]

In the 10 years from the building of the Lookout to the departure of Governor Hunter in mid-1800, some 103 ship arrivals were recorded,[70] including multiple arrivals such as that of the store ship *Britannia*. This average of one ship every 5 weeks maintained the value of a Lookout, needed now more to give advance notice to the colonial settlement of the imminent arrival than to signal to the arriving ship.

There seems to have been no new building in this area during the governorship of John Hunter which extended from 1795 to 1800, since a list of all public works was published by Collins.[71] It was the Macquarie era which left its permanent mark on South Head, with the building of a lighthouse to the south in 1816-18.

Lookout and Flagstaff with Macquarie Lighthouse 1826
SOURCE Lithograph 'Sydney lighthouse', Views in Australia, Augustus Earle, Mitchell Library,
State Library of NSW, PX*D 321, Pt. 2, no. 2

The role of the Lookout was replaced by a new Signal Station built in 1838 and continuing in use until today.

The Signal Station

From 1832 the staff at the Lookout site used a system of signal flags authorised by Harbourmaster Nicholson to send messages to Sydney and beyond. A newspaper article at the time described that near the lighthouse:

> There is also a signal-staff on this point, at no great distance from the edge of the cliff, which communicates with the telegraph at Sydney. Information of ships seen to the northward or southward is instantly given, and the town's folk are instantly apprised of a vessel approach and know what ship, where from, and the nature of her cargo, long before she makes her appearance.... But the code of signals is very great, and very ingenious, and requires a book of reference to understand and become acquainted with them.[72]

Messages were sent to Flagstaff Hill (now Observatory Hill)[73] which itself had signal connections with Parramatta via an 'Intermediate Signal station' near Kissing Point.[74]

The settlement at South Head and the nearby community of Watsons Bay was small, scattered and isolated. During 1836 the trial took place of two men for armed breaking and entering one of the houses of the signal station staff; they escaped with only food but were captured and one of them was sentenced to death.

In June 1838 the NSW Government invited tenders 'from persons willing to undertake the Mason's work required in erecting a new Signal House at South Head.'[75] This was to the design of Colonial Architect Mortimer Lewis, who had bought and developed a property at nearby Watsons Bay in 1837, selling it to the colonial treasurer Pieter Laurentz Campbell in 1839.[76] The new signal house was a stone building, represented by the two lower floors of the tower that survives today, and is shown in the advertisement for the subdivision of Campbell's land in about 1841, with a semaphore pole immediately north and a flagstaff to the north of that. The two level building was cut 3 metres into the rock from which it rose in an octagonal form to an observation level. To complete the renovation project, another tender in January 1841 was invited 'from persons willing to undertake the erection of a Flag Staff, together with certain repairs to the Semaphore, at South Head'.[77] A newspaper report in April that year noted that the repairs interrupted the visibility of the flags.[78] Adjacent staff quarters, still occupied, were built from the 1850s.

A drawing with a copy at the Signal Station shows one apparently timber hut next to the two storey signal station.[79]

Visibility was not always possible. On 20 August 1857 the Dunbar was wrecked on the rocks immediately below the Signal Station with the loss of all but one of her 121 passengers and crew.

The system of semaphore flags giving details of arriving ships,[80] was replaced in January 1858 using the first electric telegraph line in NSW,[81] which connected the Signal Station with the city.

In 1890 the building was raised to its present height of four levels with a signal lamp room above. The fourth floor provides the Signal Station staff with outlooks on all sides, and door to an outside balcony with balustrade around the building. The floor, set 85 metres about sea level, has visibility for up to 18 nautical miles. From this fourth floor observation room is access to the roof space in which is a large signal lamp.

The Sands Directory for 1892 recorded 4 staff resident at the Signal Station (only one less than at the nearby Macquarie Lighthouse): a signal master, an assistant signal master, a telegraph operator and a messenger.[82]

The primary role of the Signal Station remained to observe and report ship arrivals to the city of Sydney and to record shipping movements.[83] The register began in November 1797 – by 1998 it was recording 2800 shipping movements for the year.[84] A second function was to advise pilots of vessels arriving so they could go out to meet them; in much of the 19th century the flag announcing a ship was the signal for freelance pilots to race and compete for providing pilotage services.

In the Second World War the site was part of the military defences and was responsible for monitoring all vessels approaching Sydney Harbour.[85] But submarines were a different matter and when Japanese midget submarines entered Sydney Harbour in the night of 31 May 1942 messages were sent *to* the Signal Station, not from it, in the panic that followed the explosion at Garden Island.

Different agencies of the NSW Government took on responsibility for the Signal Station. From 1936 the responsible body was the Maritime Services Board. Ship based radio communication reduced the importance of visual observation, but the Signal Station remained to supplement and confirm this, and was especially important for smaller vessels. The MSB finally ceased to operate the Station on 23 March 1992,[86] relying on their main operation centre at Millers Point together with closed circuit cameras for visual observation.

Since that date it has remained in permanent use by volunteers initially from both the Royal Volunteer Coastal Patrol and the Australian Volunteer Coast Guard Association, and now from just the latter. They man radios and maintain visual contact every day, typically for 120 hours a week for the benefit of small and recreational boats. The site has thus maintained its role for over two centuries, and from the same building for most of that time.

South Head roads and transport

Access to South Head by water long remained the norm. But the horses in the colony increased in number:[87] from 20 in July 1794[88] to 49 in June 1795[89] to 84 at the end of 1797, 117 in 1798, 111 in 1799, 203 in late 1800. By 1802 some 293 were recorded[90] and the total grew to 517 by 1805.[91] This stimulated both the desire and the possibility to visit South Head by land.

A track used by the staff at the Lookout was improved into a road in 1803, when it was cleared to a track 15 feet wide by a contract for £100 with Surgeon John Harris. This proved an unsatisfactory construction.[92]

The 'road leading to the South Head' is marked on the October 1807 'Plan of the Town of Sydney' by Jan Meehan.[93] This was the route that led over the ridge and was later defined as Old South Head Road. Macquarie's development of the city led to a new link from Sydney to the road. This was funded largely by public subscription:

> The new road to South Head, when finished, promises to become a fashionable resort, from the accommodation it will afford to carriages, which heretofore could not possibly pass by without extreme difficulty and danger.[94]

The major work was carried out by 21 soldiers of the 73rd Regiment over a 10 week period and an obelisk extant in Watsons Bay, though possible erected a little later, records this achievement:

> 'This Road made By Subscription Was compleated in ten Weeks from the 25 of march 1811 By 21 Soldiers of His Majesty Reghtment'.

On 5 October 1811 a proclamation stated:

> a new line of road having been lately laid and completed … joins the new road, leading from thence over sand hills to the South Head, all persons are to take notice that such cars, carts or wagons as may be sent for any purpose towards the South Head Road must be sent by the new line of road leading from Pitt-street.[95]

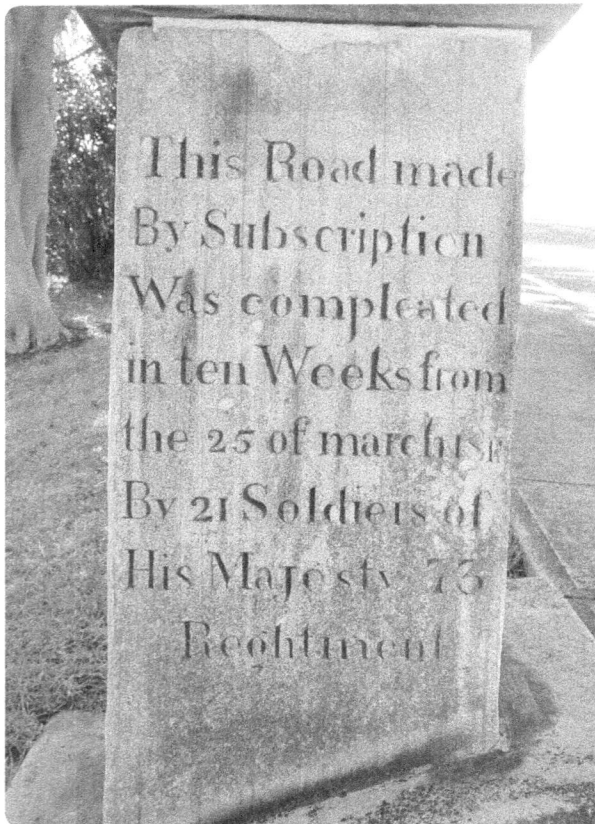

The South Head road marker, Watsons Bay
SOURCE Robin Derricourt

The role of the new road was recreation, a dramatic contrast to the business like role of the roads leading from Sydney to the challenging interior. Faro[96] has reviewed the symbolic importance of the road and its access to South Head for the colony.

By August 1812 it could be reported:

> the new road to South Head, so far as it is now carried, presents to the inhabitants of the Town a beautiful avenue of recreation, either as a pleasure ride or promenade, that attracts the wonder of the

meditating passenger who reflects, that scarce a twelvemonth has elapsed since the smooth and level course that now invites him onward, exhibited a wild, almost impenetrable ... [and so on]. [97]

By March 1813 it was noted that the road made 'for the convenience and pleasant recreation of the inhabitants of the Colony' was being damaged by carts using it to collect firewood for sale, to avoid the toll for using the Parramatta road, so a tollgate was established at the southeast corner of Hyde Park, with private users excused the toll.[98]

Despite this attempt at regulation the road became damaged by use, especially as it crossed the sandy areas between Rose Bay and Bondi Beach, which needed repairs in late 1819 or early 1820 'on account of carriages not being able to travel through as depth of sand, which at two thirds of the way knocked up the horses'. By then, according to the *Sydney Gazette*, it had again become preferable to visit South Head by water because of the poor condition of the road. Major repairs were undertaken, under the Chief Engineer Major Druitt.[99] And a result 'the whole line of road having been well covered with an excellent hard gravel…which…must secure to the town of Sydney one of the most agreeable rides that imagination could contemplate.'

South Head had thus become a favourite site for a recreational drive for the citizens of Sydney.[100]

And repairs were needed again nine years later in 1829, when the road was levelled and widened to be 'much more commodious and safe for carriages of every description'.[101]

Safety in driving had not been the only concern; a year earlier

> a gang of bushrangers, consisting it is said of ten in number, runaways from Iron Gangs, at present infest the south-head road, and the adjoining neighbourhood. Police are on the alert for their apprehension.[102]

Even a year later a servant going on the road to the 'country residence' of Robert Cooper was attached and robbed[103] – this was close to the city in Paddington rather than the country. A Francis McGlen applied in 1826 to be appointed a District Constable to combat 'bushranging…in the South Head area'.[104]

The South Head Road was noted for its access to what is now called Bellevue Hill, which gave a view back to the city which was used by artists. The less developed track near the harbour – later to be defined as New South Head Road – gave vistas above Vaucluse House from which other artists could look back up the harbour or down to South Head.[105] Both are shown on an 1832 plan,[106] but with the eastern (Old) South Head Road the better track.

Maintenance continued to be an issue for a road whose main purpose was pleasure not commerce. But the development of settlement inspired further demands. In 1831:

> The new road to South Head will be found to have been merely the means of a useless expenditure of money and labour, unless it be rendered something more

than a mere bottom of sand and stumps of trees – and it is nothing more at present … dangerous for carriages of any sort.[107]

And again in 1841:

> The Government have recently obtained excellent prices for land situated on the South Head Road [*probably closer to the city*]. It is surely the bounden duty of his Excellency to see to the improvement of many portions of this road, which are now in an almost impassable state. In several places there is no other thoroughfare than a deep and heavy sand … It is to be hoped that this improvement … Afford to the inhabitants of Sydney a convenient approach to the South Head, which would then form the object of a delightful excursion, and thus contribute to the health and enjoyment of the community.[108]

A second road near the harbour – later to be defined as New South Head Road – was developed in the 1830s. The two roads met near the Macquarie Lighthouse and terminated at the Signal Station so that visitors by land had to take a rough track down to Watsons Bay, until around 1854 when the road was extended down to the ferry and the soon to be subdivided land.

Also from 1854, the first regular ferry service (twice daily) was announced by the Sydney and Melbourne Steam Packet Company, which was by then the owner of the former Laing's grant, and the ferries docked at Victoria Wharf adjacent to this land.[109] It reverted to an irregular and excursion timetable but from 1876 a regular ferry service operated to Watsons Bay and a new wharf was built in the present location by 1881. The South Shore Steam Ferry Company (and its successor Sydney Ferries Ltd.) developed a full ferry service serving both visitors and commuters (which included school children) until 1933. Apart from excursion ferries it was not until the 1970s that regular ferries returned to Watsons Bay. A major tragedy struck in 1927 when the ferry *Greycliffe* was struck by the ocean liner *Tahiti* while on the way to Watsons Bay; over half the 40 fatalities were residents from or near Watsons Bay.

Ferry transport widened the range of citizens who could take an excursion to the area, and stimulated the growth of facilities for visitors. With the arrival of the ferry came the opening of the Marine Hotel (including its zoo) and its successors. Back on Military Road the Gap Hotel opened by the early 1860s and around 1886 the Palace Hotel (today a residential hotel and popular bar) opened near the ferry wharf. Next door a Tea Room on Marine Parade opened around 1885 (with boat hire for fishermen); it transformed into the Ozone Tea Rooms in 1908, and then became Doyle's restaurant, an iconic Sydney landmark. In 1904 the Marinato family opened a refreshment room on the wharf itself,[110] leased for 2/6 (25c) a week, and this expanded until in 1968 the Doyle family bought it. A new Gap Tavern operated from 1961 to 1997.

From 1903 the tram line brought visitors as far as the Signal Station where visitors would find the Everitt's Signal Dining Rooms and the Grand Pacific Hotel. This required a long walk down to Watsons Bay until in 1909 the tramways extended to Military Road just between the Gap and Robertson Park, with a cutting through Gap Park. The trams were discontinued in 1960 and were replaced by buses. Today Watsons Bay is one of the most visited locations in New South Wales: popular with overseas and local tourists.

Pilots

The need for pilots had a great influence on the development of Watsons Bay,[111] which remained the location for a pilot station until 2008.

The charts of Port Jackson were essential for ships to avoid shallows and obstacles such as the Sow and Pigs reef, but charts were not enough. A pilot for boats was made available at South Head as early as May 1792.[112] Collins wrote:

> a fishery was established at the South Head, exclusively for the use of the sick, under the direction of one Barton, who had been formerly a pilot, and who, in addition to this duty, was to board all ships coming into the harbour and pilot them to the settlement.

A visit of the *Minerva* in January 1800 noted 'we entered by Sydney Heads, and fired a gun for a pilot, but none appeared.'[113] A similar complaint was made in writing in September 1803 by Captain Colnett of *HMS Glatton*,[114] who records passing the flagstaff and making their own signal (presumably by firing a cannon) upon rounding the heads, with no response; he suggested there should have been a vessel at the harbour mouth both to aid ships into Port Jackson and to guard against escaping convicts. But in 1804 there were certainly 'pilots'.[115]

Watsons Bay showing pilot's house, 1810
SOURCE Alexander Hoey, Pilot's House and Watson Bay, PRO Northern Ireland D3220/2/3B

On 23 March 1809 it was announced 'the Lieutenant-Governor has been pleased to appoint Mr. Thos. Reiby to be a pilot in this harbour & c.'[116] This role was not to last long for Reiby, who had recently been travelling to India, fell sick and died in 1811. He is best known through his widow, Mary Reib[e]y, an important early business entrepreneur.

A watercolour by Alexander Hoey shows Watsons Bay from the water. It is entitled 'Pilot's House and Watson [sic] Bay' and shows Camp Cove, Green Point, a significant house set just above Watsons Bay, the signal flagstaff and the stone column with a small hut between these.[117]

This would be the house of Robert Watson. In 1811 the whole issue was addressed more seriously. Robert Watson was already living at South Head, probably undertaking some piloting duties since 1809, if not before,[118] and he was appointed in 1811 as pilot of Port Jackson[119]. It was much more logical to be based near the harbour entrance. And he gave his name to the area: that year the name Watson's Bay was first used, reporting a visit by Governor Macquarie on 9th April 1811:

> To Camp Cove, now called Watson's Bay, where the native fig tree spreads its foliage into an agreeable alcove.[120]

Robert Watson became harbourmaster in 1813, and the first keeper of the Macquarie lighthouse in 1818.

When Joseph Lycett sketched at South Head in 1818 he included 'one of the houses belonging to the pilots who are constantly stationed near the Heads for the purpose of attending vessels upon the signal of their first approach'.[121] It seems that the government allowed Robert Watson land on which he built a stone house, still standing to 1830,[122] but this was not a formal land grant of ownership.

It was, however, a quite different Watson – Captain Thomas Watson – who worked as a pilot from the inner area of Port Jackson from about 1823.[123] In the 1828 Census, when he was aged only 29, he and his wife Hannah had a significant household of servants at his Watsons Bay residence.

The other pilot was an older man, Richard Siddins. His household at the 1828 census was also well supplied with servants.

From 1833 legislation required almost all vessels to use a pilot to enter or leave Port Jackson,[124] and competition between pilots began. Land grants were made to both pilots Thomas Watson and Richard

Thomas Watson in ca. 1865-70
SOURCE Mitchell Library, State Library of NSW, P1 / 1918

Captain Cook II vessel
SOURCE Australian National Maritime Museum

Siddins in 1835 – Watson would sell his 'Marine Villa at Watson's Bay' in 1837[125] – and they had individual responsibility for offering pilotage services.

From 1840 even night-time arrivals could be supplied with a pilot, a service supplemented from 1850 by the availability of steam tugs. 1847 saw the first of the Portuguese sailors who settled in Watsons Bay and some provided pilot services as well as being fishermen.[126] The shipwreck of the *Catherine Adamson* in October 1857 while under pilot's control, two months after the offshore loss of the *Dunbar*, stimulated official review of pilotage arrangements.[127] In 1860 the Government took the initiative to buy back land to build a Pilot Station, followed by increased resources to provide pilots in all weathers.[128] The service varied between public and private control from that time,[129] as the private competitive pilots with their crews in whaleboats were complemented by steamers. For long it remained with the staff of the Signal Station to alert pilots to incoming vessels. From 1875 the Government took full responsibility for the service, initially with the steamer *Thetis* then by successive *Captain Cook* steamers. By 1948 there were ten sea pilots and three harbour pilots.[130]

The village remained the location of pilots until 25 November 2008, when the reduction of commercial shipping in Port Jackson led the Sydney Ports Corporation to relocate to Millers Point the pilots' base at Gibson's Beach on the south of Watsons Bay.

The calm water and ease of launching small boats meant that the northern end of Camp Cove was used not just by early pilots, but by the Water Police as a base, after they were relocated there in 1840 from Garden Island. The foundations of the wharf used by the Water Police from 1842 now ends in a tidal gauge. The Water Police had both residence and offices here, while a later building constructed at the end of the 19th century for military personnel and now called the Constable's Cottage occupies the same site. Following the wrecking of the *Dunbar* in 1857 a lifeboat shed was erected at the north end of Camp Cove, and volunteers manned to provide a rescue service, with a second boat shed for the Artillery in the 1890s.

Lighthouses

The staff of the signal station (Lookout) erected a signal and warning light at night for shipping at South Head, and a fee was charged to ships entering the harbour to pay for this

> in order that a light may be shewn to all vessels approaching this harbour in the night time by the guard stationed at the Signal Post, South Head[131]

but this was of limited visibility.

Lachlan Macquarie, governor of New South Wales from 1810 to 1821, initiated a proper lighthouse to replace this signal light, following a commission to Francis Greenway to evaluate sites and options.[132] In July 1816 Macquarie with the principal engineer Captain Gill laid the foundation stone for the building intended for the several purposes of a Signal and Lighthouse, and a guardhouse and barrack for a small military detachment. 'The centre of the building ... is to be raised 65 feet above the level ... the wings of the building are to form the Guard House and Barrack.'[133] It was to be named the Macquarie Tower.[134]

The First Macquarie Lighthouse
SOURCE Light House, South Head of Pt. Jackson, 'Drawings of Sydney', Mitchell Library, State Library of NSW, PX*D 123, Folio 7a

Camp Cove.

Laing's Point

Watsons Bay

E. Laing
20

Parsley Bay

Vaucluse Bay

Rob⁺ Cantell
25

Flag Staff
Outer South Head

Macquarie Tower

VII—

Thomas Laycock
80

Fra⁵ McGlyn
60

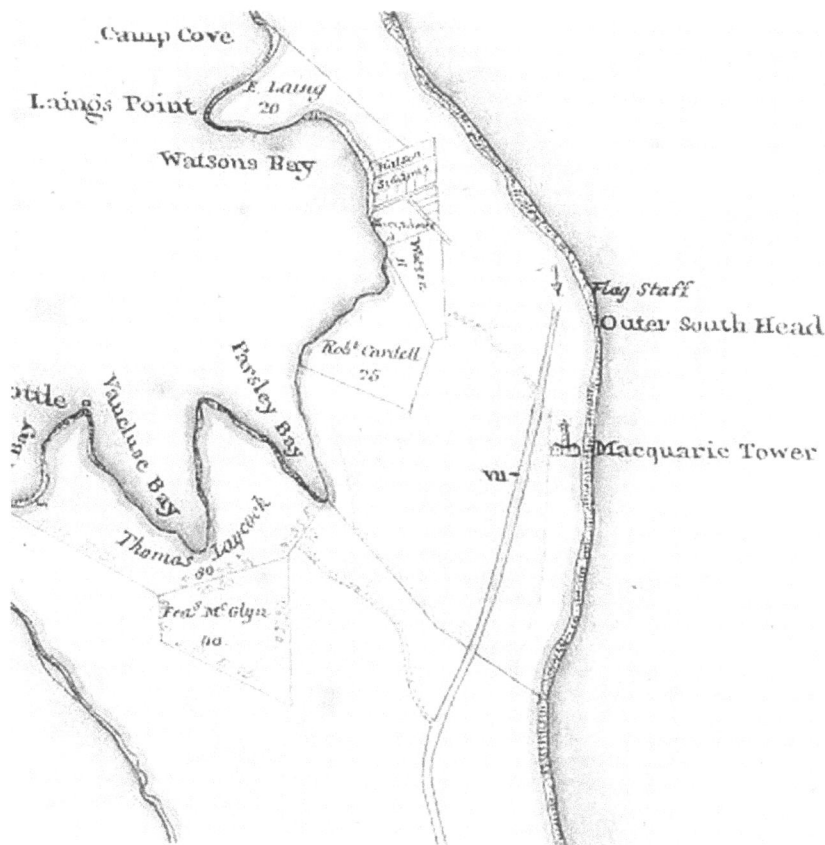

Watsons' Bay, Outer
South Head and
Vaucluse 1828
SOURCE Florence's
Trig Survey of Port
Jackson, NSW State
Records

Building of the lighthouse, designed by Francis Greenway, took two years. By November
1818

> The Macquarie tower and lighthouse at the South Head being now compleated
> and the Lanthern with revolving lights in readiness to be lighted for the benefit of
> ships or vessels arriving on the coast at night ... the lights will commence.[135]

Robert Watson, who had been harbourmaster and pilot in Port Jackson and had given his
name to 'Watson's Bay', was appointed the first Superintendent and Keeper of the Light
of Macquarie Tower, from 1818, at a salary of £50 per annum. H. Cole followed him in
November 1819[136] and in March 1822 Thomas Watson was appointed to this role,[137] also
acting as pilot from 1825,[138] and Thomas Weeland in February 1826.[139]

Thereafter it became commonplace for scenic illustrations of Sydney to be drawn or
painted from the west taking in the view across Sydney Cove, and to include in the far
distance on the horizon both the Lighthouse and the signal station's flagstaff.[140]

Just before Macquarie's return to England he proudly took his successor Sir Thomas
Brisbane to show him the lighthouse and Brisbane 'was highly pleased'.[141]

A local poet wrote a verse to celebrate the lighthouse:

Behold, on yonder cliff, a beacon shines
Whose torch-light thus a brilliant blaze displays.
It shines to guide the sea-tossed mariner
Across his trackless, rough and watery ways.[142]

A map from 1828 shows the lighthouse, flagstaff and Vaucluse House, and appears to mark an obelisk on the harbour side – perhaps the marker of the end of the road.[143]

The original lighthouse and its replacement
SOURCE Australian Maritime Safety Authority

A veranda was added around 1830, and new quarters for staff in 1836.[144] From time to time the Lighthouse was repaired and if it did not operate as expected a complaint could be expected.[145] By 1866 structural decay required serious structural repairs including straps to the tower. In 1878 work began on a replacement lighthouse with a larger light, together with new accommodation for the staff. The design was under the control of colonial architect James Barnet. Externally this was broadly a replica of the Greenway building, but with a significantly improved lens system and larger lantern giving a range of 25 miles (40 kilometres). To avoid blocking the light during construction it was erected immediately to the west so that for a while two buildings coexisted. The new light began operation in June 1883, and additional buildings for staff in 1881 and 1885, with expansion in 1899. The whole of the Greenway building was demolished by 1887. Most of the late 19th century staff quarters were demolished in 1970; today only two staff buildings remain: the Head Keeper's Quarters (1836) and the Assistant Keepers' Quarters (1881).

The 1883 lighthouse had been lit by gas-generated electricity but in 1912 this was replaced by kerosene, and in 1933 reconverted to electricity. Automation of the light limited the need for staff on site after 1976, and the last employees left in 1989.

Control of the lighthouse passed to the Commonwealth Lighthouse Service in 1915. Today the light remains fully operational, the longest continuously operating lighthouse in Australia. It is under the control of the Australian Maritime Safety Authority but the site and land around it are managed by the Sydney Harbour Federation Trust for the benefit of visitors and the community.

The need for a lighthouse closer to Inner South Head became dramatically clear in the 1850s. The merchant ship *Dunbar* hit the rocks just north of the Signal Station on the night of 20 August 1857. Attempting to turn through the heads in minimal visibility after passing the Macquarie Lighthouse, currents had kept the vessel further south than intended and it hit the rocks with the loss of all but one of its 122 passengers and crew. And two months later the *Catherine Adamson* foundered at North Head with the loss of twenty-one lives.

Hornby lighthouse (right) and Signal Station (left)
SOURCE 'South Head' by Frederick Garling, Dixson Galleries, State Library of NSW, DG SSV1 / 18

In response, urgent action was taken to mark the entrance to the harbour with another lighthouse at Inner South Head. The Hornby Light (also called the Lower Light) – painted red and white to distinguish it by day from the Macquarie Light – was operational by 1858, and named after the family of Governor Dennison's wife. Adjacent sandstone cottages for the lighthouse staff were built in 1857-1861 and extended in 1877-8. Lighting has been in turn kerosene, gas from 1904 and from 1933 unmanned automated electric light, after which the military took over the Lightkeepers' quarters.

Fortifications and military use

There have been frequent recommendations for the fortification of South Head to help defend Sydney Harbour from attack; fewer actual constructions of fortifications and even fewer installations of actual artillery, until the Second World War.[146]

In 1804 Governor King suggested

> in order to fortify the harbour it would be necessary to have a battery of twelve eighteen-pounders on the inner South Head, one side to face the east.[147]

The military road built by Governor Macquarie to Outer South Head in 1811 would allow the transport of men and equipment, if required, but no permanent garrison was established. Numerous nineteenth century reports on the defence needs of Sydney Harbour made recommendations that included the fortification of South Head, and gun emplacements at Inner South Head in particular, but action on these was slow. Reports recommended the building of a fort, the need for an observation tower, the extension of the military road to the Hornby Light, and the installation of a boom across the harbour from Inner South Head.

Some construction of fortifications at South Head may have started by 1841, but fortifications were only completed in 1854, accelerated by the threats of the Crimean War. Then defence priorities were reassessed and it seems no artillery was installed at that time. A 'Government Road to the battery' existed from the 1850s from Watsons Bay to Inner South Head.

Following the departure of British troops from the colony in 1870, work resumed on fortifications at South Head in 1871, and by 1874 there was actual artillery in place: three 10-inch, two 9-inch and five 80-pounder guns, supplemented in 1878 by torpedo firing stations at Green Point south of Camp Cove. Around 1880 a cobblestone road was constructed from Camp Cove to take equipment landed there by boat up to the fortifications above. By 1887 there was an operating room for Sydney's defences at South Head. Further south near the Signal Station a breech-loading disappearing gun was installed by the early 1890s.

At the southern end of Camp Cove stands the house built by Russian scientist Nicolai Miklouho-Maclay between 1879 and 1881 as the base for a marine biological research station. Despite the excellent location for such a venture the house was taken over in 1885 for military purposes – and became property of the Commonwealth of Australia in 1908. It was mainly used as officers' residential quarters until 2001, after which it was handed to the Sydney Harbour Federation Trust and it has seen adaptive reuse as a private residence.

At Federation there was a large but ageing array of artillery established as Sydney's defences, but by 1911 this was rationalised and with greater emphasis on South Head, which had 8 of the 20 guns in position and two more not yet mounted. Though manned in the Great War, they were given little strategic priority.

After that war the focus shifted further to South Head: in 1927 of ten guns mounted to defend Sydney Harbour, one was at the Signal Station and two at Inner South Head, with a further two mounted in reserve. The military acted to close South Head to fishermen. The School of Artillery near Gap Bluff from about 1895 to 1938 had its own practice batteries.

Sydney's Second World War defences maintained artillery both at Inner South Head (now referred to as the Hornby Batteries) and near the Signal Station, together with Green Point at Camp Cove. The Signal Station battery was dismantled soon after the war, and much of the sequence of fortifications from a century of defences remain visible and accessible to visitors.

The military training establishment HMAS Watson, lying between Inner South Head and the Gap Bluff, was established in 1945, incorporating the Naval Radar Communications Centre at Gap Bluff. From the 1950s it incorporated the Radar Training School.[148]

The boundaries of HMAS Watson include Aboriginal engraving sites together with remains of early fortifications from 1876 onwards, some with brick-lined tunnels.[149] The boundaries of HMAS Watson contain four weatherboard military barracks buildings from the period 1876-1903. The Chapel – dedicated to St George the Martyr – dates from 1961[150] and replaces an earlier tin building.

The area between Inner South Head, and Camp Cove became part of the Sydney Harbour National Park since 1977, which allowed its transformation into a recreational area.

Notes and References

1   As nautical time began at noon the previous day, this was recorded as 6 May.
2   Transcription of the National Library of Australian edition at http://southseas.nla.gov.au/journals/cook/17700506.html; J.C. Beaglehole, *The Journals of Captain James Cook on his Voyages of Discovery: The Voyage of the Endeavour 1768-1771*, Cambridge: Hakluyt Society, 1968, pp. 312-3. Spelling and punctuation are modernised in all quoted passages.
3   21 January naval time.
4   D. Collins, *An Account of the English Colony in New South Wales*, (ed. J. Collier), Christchurch: Whitcombe & Tombs, 1910, p. 11.
5   J.C. Dann (ed.), *The Nagle Journal: a diary in the life of Jacob Nagle, sailor, from the year 1775 to 1841*, New York: Weidenfeld & Nicholson, 1988, pp. 92-4.
6   *Historical Records of New South Wales (HRNSW)* vol. 1.2, p. 130.
7   Dann, *Nagle Journal*, pp. 92-4.
8   But see B. Crosson, 'Camp Cove or not Camp Cove', *Outlook* (Woollahra History and Heritage Society Newsletter), 50, 2000, pp. 6-9, which reviews uncertainty about the expedition's first landfall and camp.
9   'Entrance of Port Jackson 27 January 1788' in W. Bradley, *A Voyage to New South Wales* (MS in Mitchell Library)
10 'Port Jackson from the South Head [*sic*] leading up to Sydney; Supply sailing in', in Bradley, *Voyage*.
11 Dann, *Nagle Journal*, p. 96.
12 J. Cobley, *Sydney Cove 1789-1790*, Sydney: Angus and Robertson, 1963, p. 87.
13 Collins in J. Cobley, *Sydney Cove 1791-1792*, Sydney: Angus and Robertson, 1963, p. 12.
14 W. Tench, *Sydney's First Four Years*, (ed. L.F. Fitzhardinge), Sydney: Angus and Robertson, 1961, p. 142; Bradley, *Voyage*, 8 May 1789; V. Attenbrow, *Sydney's Aboriginal past: investigating the archaeological and historical record*, Sydney: University of New South Wales Press, 1992, pp. 21-2.
15 Bradley, *Voyage*, 29 January 1790.
16 Tench, *Sydney's First Four Years*, p. 162.
17 J. Hunter, *An Historical Journal of the Transactions at Port Jackson and Norfolk*, chapter 6. See also Bradley, *Voyage*, 20 and 29 January 1790; Cobley, *Sydney Cove 1789-1790*, pp. 131-2.
18 Tench, *Sydney's First Four Years*, p. 162.
19 The original observatory built by Lieutenant William Dawes in 1788 was on lower land to the north.
20 F.J. Bayldon, 'History of the pilotage service of Port Jackson', *Journal of the Royal Australian Historical Society*, 20 (1934): 129-162, pp. 146-8 argued for a location further south, but this would be a rough area for construction and with a poorer line of sight.
21 Casey & Lowe Pty Ltd., *Archaeological assessment Macquarie Lightstation South Head*, Report for Sydney Harbour Federation Trust, Sydney, 2005.
22 B. Smith & A. Wheeler, *Art of the first fleet and other early Australian drawings*, Melbourne: Oxford University Press & New Haven: Yale University Press, 1988, p, 79, pl. 73, being 'Views of land in the neighbourhood of Port Jackson' at the Natural History Museum London; p. 79, pl. 74 (by Raper) shows the cliffs below the Lookout.
23 Bradley, *Voyage*, 29 January 1790.
24 Nanbarry and his father had been found suffering from smallpox in a canoe in Sydney Harbour and when his father died, he was taken into the colony. Newton Fowell, Mitchell Library MLMSS 4895/1/21.
25 Bradley, *Voyage*, 7 February 1790
26 Collins, *Account*, vol. 1, chapter 9.
27 Bradley, *Voyage*, 14 February 1790, referring to a later date.
28 Journal and letters of Daniel Southwell, *HRNSW* 2, pp. 661-725.
29 Tench, *Sydney's First Four Years*, p.164.
30 Southwell writes that the Lookout man on duty 'came down' to report to him.
31 *HRNSW* 2, p. 716.
32 Southwell to Mrs Southwell, *HRNSW* 2, p. 711.
33 *HRNSW* 2, p. 717.
34 Macarthur quoted in Cobley, *Sydney Cove 1791-1792*, p. 25.
35 Collins in Cobley, *Sydney Cove 1791-1792*, pp. 91-3.
36 Southwell to Butler, *HRNSW* 2, p. 712.
37 Southwell to Butler, *HRNSW* 2, p. 713-5.
38 Collins, *Account*, vol. 1, chapter 10.
39 Tench, *Sydney's First Four Years*, 3 June 1790.
40 Phillip to Under Secretary Nepean, 22 August 1790, *HRNSW* 2, p. 394.
41 Under Secretary King to Phillip, 10 August 1792, *HRNSW* 2, p. 590.
42 Southwell in *HRNSW* 2, pp. 718-720, which associates it with a letter dated 27 July 1790; though the

actual dates of construction would place it later.

43 Collins, *Account*, Vol 1, chapter 10.
44 Waterhouse quoted in Cobley, *Sydney Cove 1789-1790*, pp. 279-284.
45 Hunter, *Historical journal*, Chapter 18.
46 This suggests the column had been located on higher ground than the Lookout, thought the huts of the Lookout staff may be implied here.
47 An incident illustrated by the Port Jackson Painter; see Smith, *Art of the first fleet*, p. 66, pl. 63-4.
48 Collins, *Account*, chapter 11. See also Tench, *Sydney's First Four Years*, p. 178; Hunter, *Historical journal*, Chapter 18.
49 Collins, *Account*, vol. 1, chapter 12.
50 Ball in Cobley, *Sydney Cove 1791-1792*, p. 169.
51 Collins, *Account*, vol. 1, chapter 17.
52 Collins, *Account*, vol. 1, cited in Cobley *Sydney Cove 1791-1792*, p. 273.
53 Tench, *Sydney's First Four Years*, p. 181.
54 Hunter, *Historical journal*, chapter 18.
55 Collins, *Account*, cited in J. Cobley *Sydney Cove 1793-1795*, Sydney: Angus and Robertson, 1983, pp. 275-6.
56 G. Aplin (ed.), *A difficult infant*, Sydney: NSW University Press, 1988, p. 13; E.C. Rowland, 'The story of the South Arm: Watson's Bay, Vaucluse and Rose Bay', *Journal of the Royal Australian Historical Society*, 37, 1951: 217-244, p. 237.
57 Collins in Cobley, *Sydney Cove 1793-1795*, p. 276.
58 Hunter to Banks in J. Cobley, *Sydney Cove 1795-1800: the second governor*, Sydney: Angus and Robertson 1986, p. 124.
59 *Sydney Gazette*, 31 March 1805.
60 *Sydney Gazette*, 5 January 1827, 11 January 1827, 16 February 1827, 17 March 1827.
61 Cobley, *Sydney Cove 1795-1800*, p. 187, quoting Collins.
62 *HRNSW* 4, p. 121.
63 *HRNSW* 6: King and Bligh 1806, 1807, 1808, p. 142.
64 *HRNSW* 6, p. 144.
65 *The Australian* 30 January 1841, p. 2; 10 April 1841, p. 2.
66 Smith, *Art of the first fleet*, p. 80, pl. 75, 'A view of the entrance into Port Jackson' by the Port Jackson Painter), and p. 81, pl. 77 'A view of the land from Botany Bay to Port Jackson' attributed to John Hunter. Given the flagstaff, both are later than the *ca.* 1788 date given by Smith and Wheeler.
67 Collins, *Account*, vol. 2, frontispiece map.
68 Smith, *Art of the first fleet* p. 136, pl. 143, 'New South Wales sketch of the settlements', 20th August 1796' by John Hunter.
69 Smith, *Art of the first fleet*, p. 75, pl. 70, 'Chart of Port Jackson New South Wales' by George Raper.
70 Collins, *Account*, vol. 2, pp 316-19.
71 Collins, *Account*, vol. 2, pp. 308-314.
72 *The Saturday Magazine*, 305, 1 April 1837, p. 124.
73 E. Walker, 'Old Sydney in the Forties', *Journal of the Royal Australian Historical Society*, 16, 1930: 292-320, p. 314.
74 W.S. Campbell, 'The Parramatta River and its vicinity 1848-1861', *Journal of the Royal Australian Historical Society*, 5, 1919: 249-283, p. 254.
75 *The Australian*, 20 June 1838, supplement p. 2.
76 Martin, *Thematic History of Watsons Bay* [manuscript in Woollahra Library Local History Collection], 1997, p. 18.
77 *The Australian*, 30 January 1841, p. 2.
78 *The Australian*, 10 April 1841, p. 2.
79 Image entitled 'The Blacksmith's Shop' by John Vine Hall, pencil sketch PXA 4461-2, State Library of NSW. Another image, of this overhang used as a blacksmith's shop dates from about 1825 by Augustus Earle: National Library of Australia pic-an2818366.
80 Bayldon, 'Pilotage service', pp. 156-7.
81 P.R. Stephensen, *The History and Description of Sydney Harbour*, Adelaide: Rigby, 1966, p. 16.
82 *Sands's Sydney and Suburban Directory for 1892*, Sydney: Sands, 1892.
83 NSW State Records Series 4586 'Arrivals and departures' 1917-1922, 4617 'Miscellaneous register relating to telegraph operations' 1914-1919, 4618 'Log books' 1918-1973, 4619 'Record of stores requested and received' 1912-1944.
84 'Signal station still keeps watch', *Sydney Morning Herald*, 20 January 1990, p. 33.
85 David Stevens, 'A Critical Vulnerability: the impact of the submarine threat on Australia's maritime defence 1915-1954', *Papers in Australian Maritime Affairs*, Figure 7.4; P. Grose, *A very rude awakening*,

Sydney: Allen & Unwin, 2007, pp. 7, 109-110.

86 'Ship-spotting tradition hits an optical nerve', *Sydney Morning Herald*, 16 January 1991, p 7; 'Old station's last signal', *Sydney Morning Herald*, 23 March 1992, p. 6.

87 Collins, *Account*, vol 2, (ed. J. Collier), pp. 74, 140, 278, 305.

88 Palmer cited in Cobley, *Sydney Cove 1793-1794*, p. 154

89 Paterson in Cobley, *Sydney Cove 1793-1795*, p. 259.

90 *HRNSW* 4, p. 820.

91 *HRNSW* 5, p. xxxi.

92 C. Faro, 'To the lighthouse! The South Head Road and place-making in early New South Wales', *Journal of the Royal Australian Historical Society*, 84(2), 1972: 109-129, p. 112.

93 *HRNSW* 6, opposite p. 366; original held in the Mitchell Library. Mentioned in *Sydney Gazette*, 25 May 1811.

94 *Sydney Gazette*, 25 May 1811.

95 *HRNSW* Vol. 7: Bligh and Macquarie 1809, 1810, 1811, p. 594 and map opposite.

96 Faro, 'To the Lighthouse'.

97 *Sydney Gazette*, 8 August 1812.

98 *Sydney Gazette*, 13 March 1813.

99 *Sydney Gazette*, 15 January 1820.

100 Faro, 'To the Lighthouse'.

101 *Sydney Gazette*, 30 April 30 1829, p. 2d.

102 *Sydney Gazette*, 23 May 1828, p. 2c.

103 *Sydney Gazette*, 23 May 1829, p. 2e.

104 Piper Papers, cited in B. Crosson, 'The McGlynn Grant', *Outlook* [WHHS Newsletter] 28, 1993: 7-10.

105 T. McCormick, *First views of Australia 1788-1825: a history of early Sydney*, Sydney, David Ell: 1987, pp. 58, 120, 160, 161, 162, 163, 240.

106 Plan of Old and New South Head Roads, County Cumberland. NSW State Records R784 (5050).

107 *Sydney Gazette*, 4 September 1834, p. 2.

108 *The Australian*, 23 January 1841, p. 2.

109 *Sydney Morning Herald*, 1 August 1854; 'Ferries to Watsons Bay' *Outlook* [WHHS Newsletter] 32, 1994, p. 4.

110 V. Marinato, *The Shop on the Wharf*, Glebe NSW: Fast Books, 1996.

111 F.J. Bayldon, 'History of the pilotage service of Port Jackson', *Journal of the Royal Australian Historical Society* 20, 1934: 129-162, provides a detailed history of pilotage. See also P. Lucher, 'Pilotage service Port Jackson,', *Port of Sydney* [Journal] 2, 1948: 33-6, 64-8; and G. Andrews, 'Sydney's Pilotage Service leaves the Bay', *Afloat Magazine*, February 2009 [available online].

112 Collins, *Account*; Aplin, *Difficult infant*, p. 12; J. Jervis (ed. V. Kelly), *The History of Woollahra*, Sydney: Municipal Council of Woollahra [n.d. 1960], p. 4.

113 Cobley, *Sydney Cove 1795-1800*, p. 376.

114 *HRNSW* 5, pp. 207-8.

115 They were mentioned by Governor King, *HRNSW* 6, p. 142.

116 *HRNSW* 7, p. 86.

117 Public Record Office of Northern Ireland D3220/2/3B; reproduced in McCormack, *First Views*, p. 142, which suggests it is dated about 1810.

118 Bayldon, 'History of the pilotage service', p. 131.

119 'Watson, Robert (1756–1819), *Australian Dictionary of Biography* [available online].

120 *Sydney Gazette*, 13 April 1811; discussed J.H. Watson, 'Origin of names in Port Jackson', *Journal of the Royal Historical Society*, 4, 1917-19: 361-385, p. 368.

121 J. Lycett, *Views in Australia*, London: Souter, 1824.

122 Jervis, *History of Woollahra*, p. 7.

123 Bayldon 'History of the pilotage service', p. 131.

124 Bayldon 'History of the pilotage service', p. 132; Lusher, 'Pilotage service'.

125 Watson, 'Origin of names', p. 368.

126 Jervis, *History of Woollahra*, p. 5.

127 Bayldon 'History of the pilotage service', pp. 133-4.

128 For a personal account of the 1860s see E.W. Blakeney, 'Memoirs', *Royal Historical Society of Queensland Journal*, 17(3), 1999, pp. 136-144.

129 B Crosson, 'The Pilot Station', *Outlook* [WHHS Newsletter], 39, 1997: 7-8.

130 Lusher, 'Pilotage service'.

131 *Sydney Gazette*, 22 April 1815; Watson, 'Origin of names', p. 369 notes a ship's log recording the light on 15 September 1815.

132 Rowland, 'Story of the South Arm', p. 233.

133 *Sydney Gazette*, 13 July 1816; *Sydney Gazette*, 20 July 1816 adds that it was planned to include a frieze representing the four winds.

134 For detailed topographical information and background see Casey, *Archaeological assessment*.

135 *Sydney Gazette*, 28 November 1818, p. 1.

136 *Sydney Gazette*, 13 November 1819.

137 Payment records in *Sydney Gazette*; that of 6 October 1825 also records labourers' costs.

138 *Sydney Gazette*, 24 March 1825, p. 1.

139 *Sydney Gazette*, 22 April 1826, p. 3.

140 T. McCormick, *First views of Australia*, p. 218 and passim.

141 *Sydney Gazette*, 1 February 1822.

142 *Sydney Gazette*, 16 July 1827.

143 Florence's Trig Survey of Port Jackson, NSW State Records CGS13859, map no 4752.

144 Casey, *Archaeological assessment*.

145 *The Australian*, 26 December 1826, 24 February 1830, 8 February 1840, p. 2.

146 P. Oppenheim, *The Fragile Forts: the fixed defences of Sydney Harbour 1788-1963*, Loftus: Australian Military History Publications, 2005 details both the history of policy and the actual gun emplacements; see also G.C. Wilson, *Sydney Harbour Fortifications Archival Study*, MS for NPWS, 1985.

147 *HRNSW* 6, pp. 142, 144.

148 *South Head - draft conservation management plan*, Sydney, NPWS, 2007, posted at http://www.nationalparks.nsw.gov.au/npws.nsf/Content/southhead_cmp_draft.

149 *South Head - draft conservation management plan*.

150 http://www.navy.gov.au/establishments/watson/chapelhistory.html.

3

The Development of Watsons Bay

The development of the settlement of Watsons Bay is marked by three groups of residents: government officials, people with local trades (such as fishermen) and members of the colonial elite, together with families and servants or other employees.

In the early years of the Colony it was the government officials who characterised the area; increased during the Macquarie era, which lasted from 1810 until 1821.

The creation of a community[1]

While most of the land of the South Head peninsula remained unallocated, there were rare land grants, not all taken up actively. Lieutenant-Governor Francis Grose on 12 February 1793 made a grant of 20 acres 'on the south side of the harbour at Camp Cove'[2] to Edward Laing, Surgeon in the New South Wales Corps, thus creating the alternate name of Laing's Point for what was more commonly called Green Point at the southern end of Camp Cove. But Laing did not occupy it and in October 1794 he accepted another land grant of 100 acres at Bulanaming southwest of the city.[3] He sold his holding to Thomas Laycock.[4] It was sold on in 1795 to Mr Dell then to William Wright Bampton in 1795; and inherited by his son.

By 1822 the only land allocations in this part of the colony were those of Laing's Point, the government area of Watson's Bay itself (marked as a single grant on Stewart's 1822 plan),[5] and the Vaucluse estate. To the west lay the grant at Point Piper, with grants near Coogee in the south.

The first private settlement in the peninsula was the house and estate named Vaucluse, built by Sir Henry Browne Hayes, a wealthy Irish convict[6] who was transported, arriving in 1802, being pardoned in 1809 and returning home in 1812. In 1803 he acquired at auction[7] land that had been granted in 1793 to Thomas Laycock (80 acres) and in 1795 to Robert Cardel[1] (25 acres), both subsequently transferred to Thomas Dennett in 1797. This estate of 105 acres Hayes named Vaucluse (perhaps after the village in southern France). He built a small house[8] and developed a garden.[9] William Wentworth acquired

Watsons Bay and South Head 1822
SOURCE Joseph Lycett 'View of the Heads at the entrance to Port Jackson', from 'Views of Australia, London, 1824.

the property in 1827 and developed the residence of Vaucluse House, acquiring an adjacent 370 acre grant of land to the east in 1836-38. He then sought to divide the estate and sell off blocks for development as a village of Vaucluse,[10] but the venture had little success at the time. The development of settlement between Watsons Bay and the Vaucluse estate dates mainly from the early 20th century. Wentworth's family retained possession of Vaucluse House itself until 1910 when ownership was acquired by the state.

Joseph Lycett created art that began the romantic visual image of the Watsons Bay area. His 'Distant Views of Sydney from the Light House at South Head'[11] was 'drawn from the window of the room immediately under the tower …. Frequently visited by the Governor'. His 'View of the Heads, at the entrance into Port Jackson, New South Wales',[12] also from sketches made about 1818, shows the flagstaff (quite low), a man and a horseman, a large house south of Watsons Bay itself, and another small house near it, described as belonging to a pilot. Watsons Bay is quite open but no other houses are visible.

We have two images of the area drawn by James Wallis between 1816 and 1819[13] and published in 1821.[14] One shows Vaucluse Bay from the harbour, with a small building visible. The other, with the decorative additional of Aborigines, is from the same area looking to the Heads.

The 1828 census listed some three dozen residents at Watsons Bay and South Head: mainly the families and servants of the pilots and the staff of the Signal Station and the Lighthouse, and the soldier Humphrey Humphreys, as well as labourers working these sites.

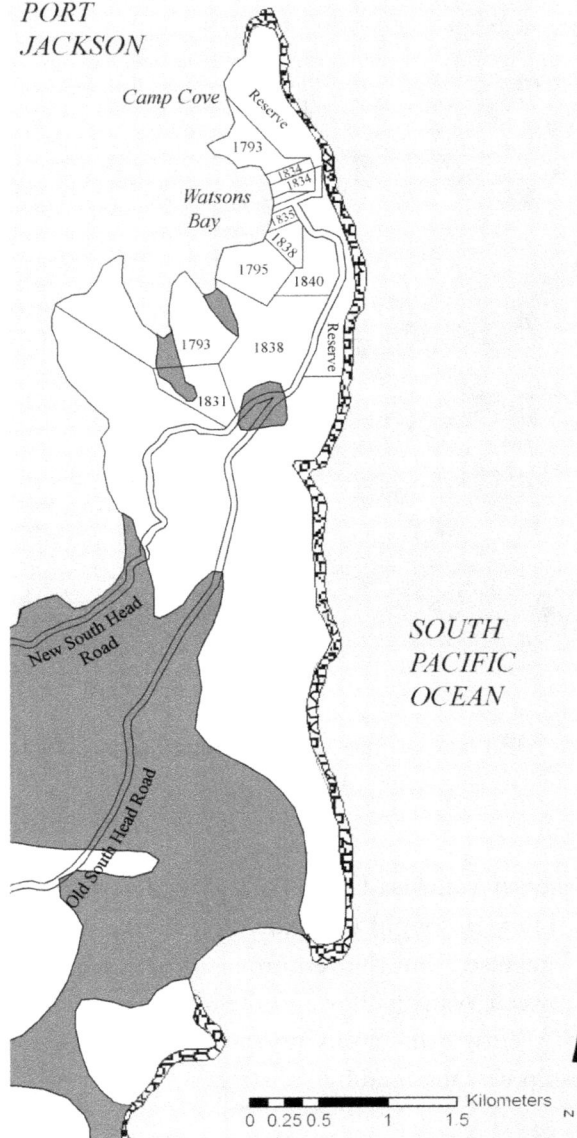

PORT JACKSON

Camp Cove

Reserve

1793

1834
1834

Watsons Bay

1835

1828

1795   1840

1793   1838

Reserve

1831

New South Head Road

SOUTH PACIFIC OCEAN

Old South Head Road

Kilometers
0 0.25 0.5   1   1.5

N

Early land grants around Watsons Bay
SOURCE Derricourt, 'South Head peninsula'

The land south of Laing's grant, to the east and south of Watsons Bay beach itself, apart from some government reserves, was from the 1830s gradually disposed of in land grants whose subsequent subdivision marked the development of the suburb of Watsons Bay and its extension towards Vaucluse.[15]

From north to south were granted formally in 1834 2.5 acres to Thomas Watson and 3.5 acres to Richard Siddins (Siddons, Siddens) – the two pilots already living there since the 1820s.[16] Other grants were 4 acres to Patrick Humphries in 1835 and 8 acres (including where the Pilot Station stood) to Thomas Horton James in 1838. Between here and the reserve for the Signal Station were 39 acres allocated to Francis Mitchell in 1840. These two plots abutted the earlier grant of 25 acres to Robert Cardel(l) east of Parsley Bay, beyond which lay Wentworth's additional vast grant of 370 acres. A grant to John Foreman in 1831 was sold on to pilot Thomas Wealands in 1839.[17]

Thomas Watson, master mariner and pilot, built a 'marine villa' on his 1834 land grant – the site of today's Robertson Park – but rented and then sold it to Hannibal Hawkins Macarthur, nephew of John Macarthur, from 1837/8 and it he named it Clovelly.[18] In 1848 it was sold to Henry Watson Parker, son-in-law of John and Elizabeth Macarthur and future premier of New South Wales. From 1864 Clovelly was occupied (and later bought) by (Sir) John Robertson, several times premier of NSW. Clovelly fell into disrepair and was eventually demolished in 1903.[19] The site and adjacent area were resumed by the government and became today's Robertson Park, mainly recreational but in World War II containing an air raid shelter.

On Richard Siddins' grant a substantial house was built by colonial architect Mortimer Lewis from 1837, renamed Zandoliet or Zandvliet when bought in 1839 by Colonial Treasurer Pieter Laurentz Campbell. In 1841 the estate of Campbell was subdivided into 17 lots for auction,[20] with unsold lots auctioned again in 1847: 'admirably adapted for marine villa residences … occupies the most central spot in that far-famed picturesque part of Port Jackson Harbour'. Alongside the establishment of pleasure steamers to Watsons Bay the main house was redeveloped as the Marine Hotel (with a restaurant) in 1854-5. In 1859 new owner Henry Billing renamed it the Greenwich Pier Hotel – and it had its own adjacent wharf. More unusually he created a private zoo for visitors, including two lions and some zebras said to have been put into harness. In time it was renamed the Royal Hotel, and an open air cinema operated behind the house. From 1924 it was used as the Town Hall for Vaucluse Council until the Council was abolished in 1948. It then took on its role as a wedding and reception centre, initially called Fisherman's Lodge and subsequently renamed as today's Dunbar House.[21]

Village growth was marked by development and subdivision. A property named Bota Foga 'extending from the Lighthouse to the waters of Port Jackson' was sold in 1836 in lots for further development, as was the property of Tivoli.[22]

In 1843 the area north of Watson's Bay itself (behind Camp Cove) which formed the grant originally given to Edward Laing (and also referred to as Roddam Farm) was subdivided and offered for sale by its then owner Judge Dennithorne, but this offer was not successful. The estate was acquired by R.M. Robey in 1854, and in 1855 the land was subdivided into 141 lots and auctioned in 1855-6 for development, but some of the lots remained unsold.[23] Robey's plan, alongside business colleague Elias Carpenter Weekes, was an ambitious one for the development of a whole new community; they were directors of the steamship company which established a ferry from the city to Victoria Street in the intended new suburb, and they had also acquired the building which became the Marine Hotel. Although their plan at this time failed – and the ferry was suspended – the plots did sell gradually over the next decades, and the Watsons Bay Village known today took shape.

Henry Watson Parker who bought Clovelly in 1848 acquired in 1851 a small grant northeast of the Thomas Watson grant, and he further expanded his holdings by buying

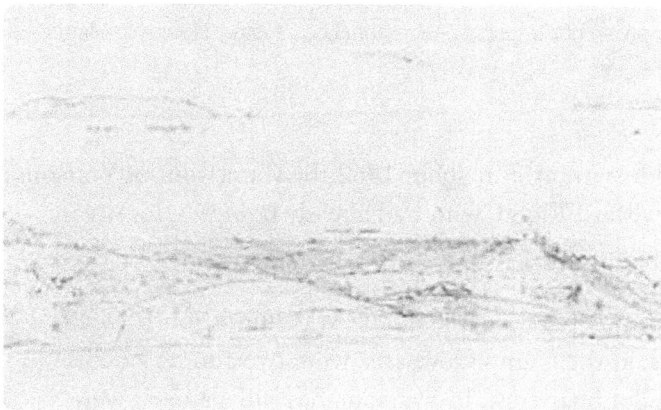

Watsons Bay 1845
SOURCE George Angus 'Sydney from Camp Cove and Sydney Harbour', National Library of Australia

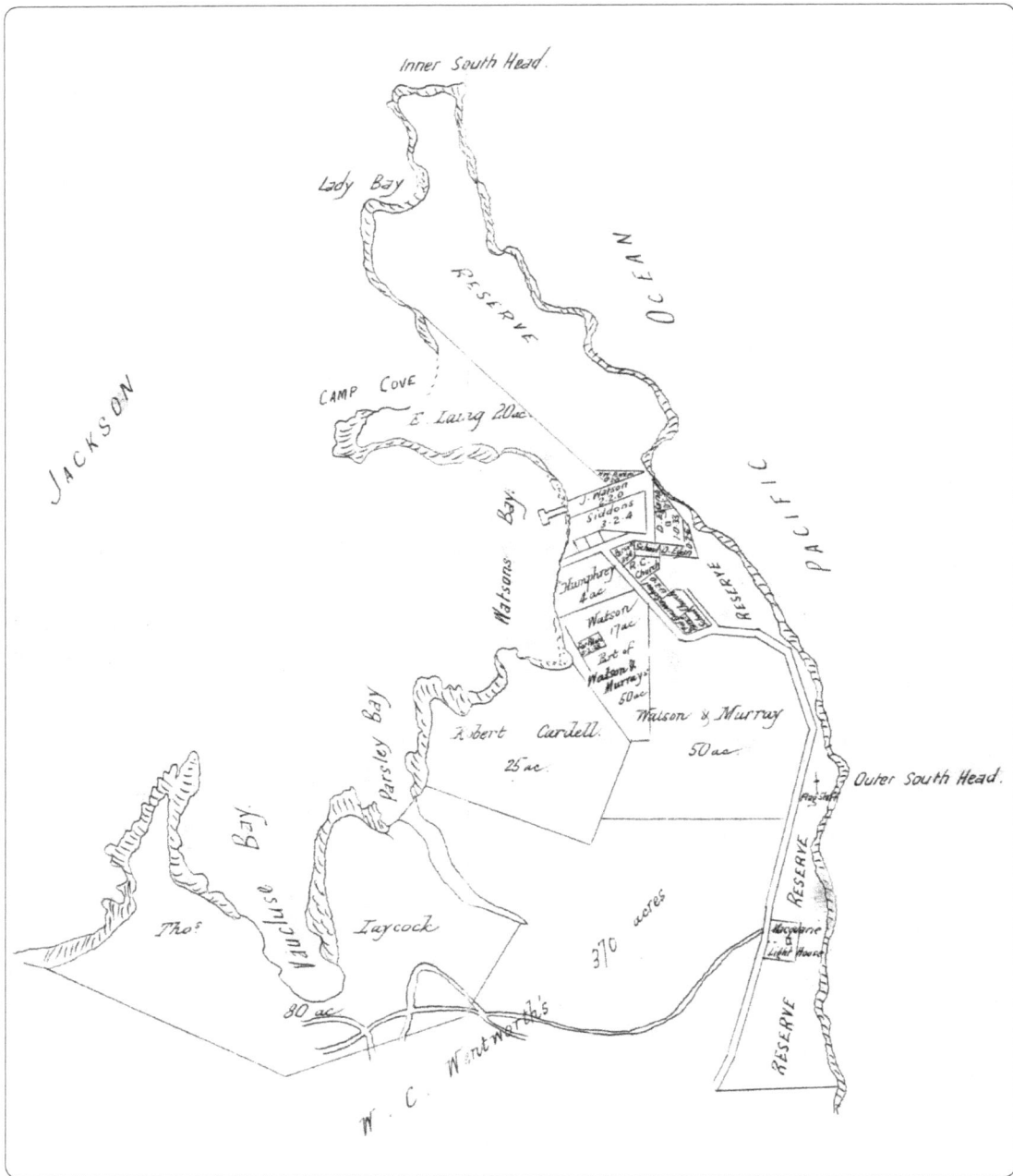

Watsons Bay subdivision

SOURCE 'Tracing shewing land at Watsons Bay parish of Alexandria", Woollahra Local History Library, in Martin, 'Thematic History'

into both the Laing grant and the Siddins grant. Finally in 1862 the waterfront of Watsons Bay was subject of an acquisition by Edward Flood, who had already bought Clovelly in 1862.[24]

The 1841 census records 13 households with 122 people in all. At (Outer) South Head were two stone and two timber houses; at the Camp Cove area were two timber houses and a tented accommodation for the pilot boat crew. In Watsons Bay village itself were listed just six households: one timber house and five stone houses.

Dated 1845 is a drawing by George Angas appears to be from Camp Cove looking south to Watsons Bay. This drawing shows about 13 houses with some additional hut outbuildings.[25]

The community in 1858 was still small. The first Sands Directory listed for that year 14 heads of households. 4 were at South Head (including the owner of the Signal Hotel, the signalmaster and the lighthouse superintendent), and the 10 listed at Watsons Bay included Henry Clay of the Marine Hotel, pilots Fullerton, Gibson, Jenkins, Kelly and Robson; and dignitaries Daniel Egan MLC and the Hon Henry Watson Parker, until the previous year Premier of the State.[26]

The great colonial artist Eugene von Guérard has a romantic view of the area 'Sydney Heads'[27] painted in 1860 from sketches made in 1859 and with several versions extant. The location is above the track at the top of the Vaucluse House estate (New South Head Road).

South Head and
Watsons Bay 1859
SOURCE von Guérard,
'Sydney Heads', lithograph

The detail cannot be taken as historically exact. In the Watsons Bay area are shown the Hornby Lighthouse, two houses at Camp Cove, at Watsons Bay itself the wharf and house both near the wharf and above the bay – two to the north, four at the wharf and four to the east, as well as the Lookout at the signal station. Paintings by Conrad Martens ('The Gap'), George Peacock and others reflect the same romantic imagery of what had now become a village of significance.

The population grew from 122 in 1841 to a recorded population of 237 people in 1868, including servants and family members.[28] The Sands directory of 1880[29] showed a much larger and more varied society: some 64 households, with three churches, a school, the artillery barracks and associated officers' quarters, and shops including grocers, a post office, three hotels; even a resident ranger in the recreation reserve. The population ranged from fishermen and a bricklayer to Sir John Robertson, the past and future Premier of New South Wales.

| Sir John Robertson

Robertson was a substantial landowner in the area; in 1887 he subdivided the area around the Gap Hotel for sale as residential plots: the future Gap Road, Dunbar Street and frontage of Military Road.

As subdivisions continued and the number of houses grew, the size of most of those households reduced, so that the 2006 Census recorded just 691 residents of Watsons Bay in 241 occupied private dwellings.

The growth of civil government and military use, residence and visitors had its impact on the landscape. Images of Watsons Bay, The Gap and South Head from the mid 19th century onwards show barren rocky treeless wastes stretching between buildings, while livestock browsed. Today's rich natural vegetation and parks are the effort of recent decades and changed ownership of open spaces.

The class mix of Watsons Bay continued long into the 20th century. Expensive modem houses, the equivalent of the 19th century 'marine villas', continued to be built alongside the small weatherboard cottages originally occupied by fishermen, government officials (including now the military) and local traders. An artistic community was also drawn to this area. Famous residents included novelist Christina Stead who used the area in her writings. Some families remained in Watsons Bay across several generations but property prices and the high value of land in the area have made a gradual and irreversible transition. The heritage value of Watsons Bay has been reflected in successive planning strategies adopted (if not always strictly applied) by Woollahra Municipal Council.

Watsons Bay in the 19th century was an hour by horse and carriage and half an hour by boat from Sydney. Even the growth of ferries and trams was focussed on the needs of day visitors, as much as residents. Until the development of private car ownership, local shops therefore served the needs of the residents of Watsons Bay and in the 20th century those of the growing population of adjacent Vaucluse (a suburb which grew to thirteen times the population of Watsons Bay). At different times Watsons Bay had its own bakery, butchery, general store, haberdashery, barber, pharmacy, newsagent and fuel merchant, even service station. There had been a part time post office from 1854 and a permanent building from 1889 to 1988.

The church history of Watsons Bay is unusual in its origins, starting with a non-conformist chapel and then balanced between Anglican and Roman Catholic establishments.[30]

In 1839 there began by public subscription the creation of an independent chapel near the Lighthouse at South Head,[31] inspired by Richard Siddins who had Congregational church leanings. It was opened at a ceremony on 18 July 1840 at which one of the speakers was a Samoan chief, Leatona.[32] A subsequent Congregational church operated in the heart of Watsons Bay commercial area from 1891 to 1910.

Significant and neighbouring areas of Watsons Bay were allocated to the Anglican and Roman Catholic churches. In 1849 two acres were set aside for the Catholic church, especially to serve the community of Portuguese descent. The church took some time to build and was fully completed only by 1881. In 1910 it was replaced by Our Lady Star of the Sea, which was improved with choir gallery and new facade in 1940 and further changes in 1965-6.

Support for an Anglican church dates from 1847,[33] but it took until 1864 to build and consecrate the church of St Peter's (designed by Edmund Blackett) on the site to the southeast of the Catholic church. It came to serve the expanding professional classes occupying the new suburb of Vaucluse. The church hall from 1911 and the rectory from 1925 were added to the site as were the gates dedicated to the memory of those killed in the *Greycliffe* ferry and completed in 1929, when St Peter's became a full parish.

A privately run school operated in Watsons Bay in the late 1840s. Following efforts of local residents a new school was opened in 1859 – the South Head School. It was funded

The subdivision 1887
SOURCE Watsons Bay subdivision plans, Mitchell Library, State Library of NSW, SP/ W5/21.

but not initially owned by the state's school authorities. In 1877 a school opened on Old South Head Road between Catholic and Anglican churches, for up to 100 pupils, but pressure of numbers grew. A separate Catholic convent school operated for a period next door in 1907. With further suburban growth a new Vaucluse School was opened in 1925 and the old school changed to become a Scout and Guide centre and was renamed the Gunyah.

In the early years of the colony, Watsons Bay was of interest to the government because of its location: the site for staff of the lookout and Signal Station, for the lighthouses, for pilots and the water police. Its military importance grew with the fortification of South Head at intervals from 1854. Land grants were initially given to public servants whose role brought them to this extreme end of the town. The development of a mixed and larger community, especially after the subdivision of Laing's grant behind Camp Cove, brought the area's development more into the sphere of Woollahra Municipality (established 1860). But with the growth of housing in adjacent Vaucluse, a Vaucluse Municipality was established from 1895, continuing until being remerged with Woollahra in 1948. It took over the site of the former Gap Hotel in 1910 as the new Town Hall. This site remained in use until the move into Dunbar House in 1924. After that date the site was acquired by the Vaucluse Masonic Lodge and in 1926 divided into a Masonic Hall, and a Cinema on Military Road.

Conclusion

The South Head peninsula is marked by its physical characteristics: steep cliffs facing the ocean from the entrance to Port Jackson, past the Gap, to meet the sea at Bondi; on the other side, harbour coves traversed by freshwater streams. Its logistical and military importance to the administration in Sydney brought its first European settlers and supplanted the economic importance the area had to the Aboriginal community. But the village of Watsons Bay created within the peninsula broadened the settlement from fishermen's cottages to state premiers' grand homes, and supported the whole range of community institutions: shops, churches, school, post office, and cinema. Its role grew as a favourite recreational location for Sydney residents, and eventually those from much further afield, brought by tram or ferry or bus when these replaced carriage or private boat, and in turn supporting hotels and eating places, even a small zoo, and a busy beach in Camp Cove. Behind the visual heritage of recreational reserves, lighthouses and weatherboard cottages, and foundations of fortifications, extends the history of one of the oldest European settlements in Australia and before that a heritage of intensive Aboriginal economic use.

Notes and References

1   A detailed study of ownership patterns and suburban growth was undertaken by Megan Martin, *Thematic History of Watsons Bay*, 1997; a manuscript copy is as the Local History Centre of Woollahra Library.

2   *HRNSW* 2, p. 35; Cobley, *Sydney Cove 1793-1795*, Sydney: Angus and Robertson, 1983, p. 41 cited as grant 111 of 28 May 1793.

3   MS cited in Cobley, *Sydney Cove 1793-1795*, p. 198. Robert Watson gained a grant of 30 acres in Lane Cove at the same time. In G. Cannon, *The First Titleholders of Land in the County of Cumberland* (privately published, 2 vols. 1997) Edward Laing had a 20 acre grant in Portion 398, and a 100 acre grant in 'the Parish of Petersham' portion number 152.

4   J.H. Watson, 'Origin of names in Port Jackson', *Journal of the Royal Historical Society*, 4, 1917-19: 361-385, p. 366.

5   'Plan of allotments granted from the Crown in the County of Cumberland New South Wales', NSW State Records C369a (1692).

6   *Australian Dictionary of Biography*: http://www.adb.online.anu.edu.au/biogs/A010486b.htm

7   Auction announced in *Sydney Gazette*, 10 July 1803; Laycock's 100 acres were mostly in cultivation, while about 1 acre of Cardel's 30 acres was cleared.

8   'Vaucluse beyond Port Jackson, New South Wales' ca. 1815-17, engraved from a drawing by Captain Wallis, shows this house: T. McCormick, *First views of Australia 1788-1825: a history of early Sydney*, Sydney, David Ell: 1987, p. 188.

9   http://www.hht.net.au/museums/vaucluse_house/guidebook; Watson, 'Origin of names', pp. 370-2.

10   B. Crosson, 'The village at Vaucluse', *Outlook* [WHHS Newsletter] 81, 2011: 10-12.

11   Joseph Lycett, *Views in Australia*, published in 1825, but drawn earlier; a watercolour is in the Mitchell collection 'East view of Sydney, New South Wales, taken from the Macquarie Tower, 1819'.

12   Lycett, *Views in Australia*.

13   R. & T. Rienits, *Early artists of Australia*, Sydney: Angus and Robertson 1963, p. 193.

14   Major James Wallis, *An historical account of the colony of New South Wales and its dependent settlements*, London: Rudolph Ackermann, 1821.

15   Martin, *Thematic history;* Rowland, 'Story of the South Arm'; B. Cross, 'The Watson Grants;, *Outlook* [WHHS Newsletter], 33,1995: 9-10; Crosson, 'Clovelly'; J. Jervis (ed. V. Kelly), *The History of Woollahra*, Sydney: Municipal Council of Woollahra [n.d. 1960], pp. 7-9; W. Mayne-Wilson, 'Robertson Park: its secret past', *Historic Environment* 17, 2004: 33-37; *Sydney Gazette*, 27 February 1836, p. 1; 19 March 1836, p. 1; 16 April 1836, p. 1; 21 April 1836, p. 1; 22 October 1836, p. 1; 27 October 1836, p. 4.

16   Mayne-Wilson, 'Robertson Park'.

17   Jervis, *History of Woollahra*, p. 7.

18   B. Crosson, 'Clovelly – Watsons Bay', *Outlook* [WHHS Newsletter] 16, 1989): 8.

19   Jervis, *History of Woollahra*, p. 9.

20   *The Australian*, 3 June 1841, p. 3; 29 June 1841, p. 3; 26 June 1841, p. 3; *Sydney Gazette*, 6 December 1841, p. 1.

21   Jervis, *History of Woollahra*, p. 8.

22   *Sydney Gazette*, 27 February 1836, p. 1, 19 March 1836, p. 1, 16 April 1836, p.1, 21 April 1836, p.1, 27. October 1836, p. 4, 22 October 1836, p.1, 3 November 1836, p. 4.

23   Jervis, *History of Woollahra*, p. 10.

24   B. Crosson, 'Clovelly'.

25   George French Angas, *Sketchbook* in National Library of Australia, nla pic-an 2900745.

26   *Sands and Kenny's Commercial and General Sydney Directory for 1858-9*, Sydney: Sands & Kenny, 1858.

27   National Gallery of Victoria, Accession no. A3-1986.

28   Jervis, *History of Woollahra*, p. 14.

29   *Sands's Sydney and suburban directory for 1880*, Sydney: John Sands, 1880.

30   Martin, *Thematic history*.

31   *Sydney Gazette*, 1 August 1839, p. 2; 10 October 1839, p. 2.

32   *Sydney Gazette*, 18 July 1840, p. 2.

33   C. J. Sisley, *St Peter's Church Watson's Bay*, Sydney: St Peter's Church, 1964, 2nd edition 1977.

Chronology of Development
South Head and Watsons Bay

Lookout house January 1790 –; other huts ('whitewashed') lower down and garden 1790 -

Flagstaff January 1790; replaced with larger Flagstaff June 1792; rebuilt summer 1796-97; replaced with taller one in March 1805; repaired 1827, replaced 1841

Column planned July 1790, built from September 1790; built; rebuilt after collapse August 1795

South Head Road constructed 1803, Old South Head Road reconstructed 1811, repaired 1819-20, repaired 1829, New South Head Road improved by 1832; roads extended to inner South Head 1850s

Vaucluse house and garden 1803; Wentworth developments from 1827

Macquarie Lighthouse begun July 1816, completed November 1818, repaired 1826, 1830, staff quarters 1836, new lighthouse built from 1878, operational 1883, new staff quarters 1881, 1885, 1899

Pilot's house by 1818, pilot station built 1860-62

Land grants Laing 1793 (not settled), Thomas Watson (1834), Richard Siddins (1834), Patrick Humphries (1835), Thomas James (1838), Francis Mitchell (1840), Henry Watson Parker (1851), Edward Flood (1862)

Sale (subdivision) of land from 1836

Siddins Grant: Mortimer Lewis house 1837; subdivided 1841; Marine Hotel 1854-5; Vaucluse Town Hall 1924-1949; now Dunbar House.

Signal Station built 1838, staff quarters 1850s, increased height 1890

Chapel opened July 1840, Anglican church 1864, Catholic church 1881, rebuilt 1910, Congregational chapel 1891

Water police wharf 1842

Fortifications 1854, 1871- , Artillery School 1895, HMAS Watsons 1945

Ferry service 1854, resumed 1876, new wharf 1881

Subdivision of Laing's grant 1855 to create suburb

Hornby Lighthouse built 1857/58, houses 1857-61, 1877-78

Marine Biological Research Station 1879-1881; officers' quarters 1885